ROMANTIC SHAKESPEARE

Quotes from the Bard on Love and Lovers

ROMANTIC SHAKESPEARE

Quotes from the Bard on Love and Lovers

GRAMERCY BOOKS
NEW YORK

This 1999 edition is published by Gramercy Books™,
an imprint of Random House Value Publishing, Inc.,
201 East 50th Street, New York, New York 10022.

Gramercy Books™ and colophon are trademarks of
Random House Value Publishing, Inc.

Random House
New York • Toronto • London • Sydney • Auckland

Printed and bound in the United States of America

*Compiled, edited, designed, and composited by
Frank J. Finamore*

Library of Congress Cataloging-in-Publication Data
Shakespeare, William, 1564–1616.
Romantic Shakespeare : quotes from the Bard on love and lovers.
        p.   cm.
    "Compiled, edited, and designed by Frank J. Finamore"—T.p.
verso.
    ISBN 0-517-19452-X
    1. Shakespeare, William, 1564–1616 Quotations.   2. Love
Quotations, maxims, etc.   I. Finamore, Frank J.   II. Title.
PR2771.F56   1999
822.3'3—dc21   99-27176
                                                        CIP

8   7   6   5   4   3   2   1

CONTENTS

*L*ove is perhaps humanity's ultimate mystery in life—for who knows what comes in the hereafter. Love and romance fascinate us as nothing else. If one is not in love, one wants to be in love. And as evidenced by our culture's films, television shows, and books, there is an endless parade of romantic dramas and comedies that endeavor to fill our insatiable appetite for love. This desire seems to be an essential part of our human nature, perhaps the *essential* human quality, for can anyone truly *live* without love? And storytellers and writers since the beginning of civilization have tried to understand, depict, and explain love to the clearly befuddled but fascinated masses. But do we know anymore today than we did, let's say two thousand years ago, or even four hundred years ago, the time of Shakespeare? The answer is clearly "no." Therein perhaps lies the fascination. No matter how far we delve into love's mysteries, we never will understand its truest essence, as it is as protean as one of Shakespeare's greatest characters, Cleopatra, whose description can clearly be applied to love itself—"Age cannot wither her, nor custom stale / Her infinite variety."

Love cannot be measured, quantified, or dissected, for it is this undefinable emotion that usually beggars description, except in the hands of the world's greatest poets and writers. And William Shakespeare, the English language's greatest poet and dramatist, is unrivaled when it comes to love and romance. For proof, one would just need to read the selections contained in this volume. Besides the great poetry, Shakespeare creates memorable characters in the throes of love's passion. Who in Western culture has not heard of Romeo and Juliet? They are the apotheosis of what a romantic couple should be. They stand in our imaginations as the beacons of the possibility of what love *can* be.

And Shakespeare's cast of lovers seems almost endless and range from the comic, almost farcical, sparring of Petruchio and Katharina—in *The Taming of the Shrew*—to the dark tragic love of Othello and Desdemona to the richly nuanced depiction of a more mature romance of the title characters in *Antony and Cleopatra*. What all of Shakespeare's greatest lovers have in common is that they are all people who "loved not wisely but too well." For love is a passion that cannot be denied, as he writes, "stony limits cannot hold love out," or be argued with in a rational way, as Bottom in *A Midsummer Night's Dream* notes, "reason and love keep little company together nowadays." And passionate love is something Shakespeare himself seems to have experienced in a painful way. While we may not know the exact circumstances or reasons that occasioned the writing of the *Sonnets*, the poems themselves reveal a man in the grip of love, tormented, seduced, and grappling with its ecstasies and sometimes emotionally devastating consequences.

While the only way to truly understand the genius that is Shakespeare is to read his works in their entirety, the selections herein comprise a guided tour through the gallery of some of his greatest creations as well as his incredible poetry. Reading these lines, one cannot help but to be inspired by love's burning flame.

Frank James Finamore

New York
1999

VALENTINE

> To be in love, where scorn is bought with groans;
> Coy looks with heart-sore sighs; one fading
>   moment's mirth
> With twenty watchful, weary, tedious nights:
> If haply won, perhaps a hapless gain;
> If lost, why then a grievous labour won;
> However, but a folly bought with wit,
> Or else a wit by folly vanquishèd.

PROTEUS

> So, by your circumstance, you call me fool.

VALENTINE

> So, by your circumstance, I fear you'll prove.

PROTEUS

> 'Tis love you cavil at: I am not Love.

VALENTINE

> Love is your master, for he masters you:
> And he that is so yokèd by a fool,
> Methinks, should not be chronicled for wise.

PROTEUS

> Yet writers say, 'As in the sweetest bud
> The eating canker dwells, so doting love
> Inhabits in the finest wits of all.'

VALENTINE

> And writers say, 'As the most forward bud
> Is eaten by the canker ere it blow,
> Even so by love the young and tender wit
> Is turn'd to folly, blasting in the bud,
> Losing his verdure even in the prime
> And all the fair effects of future hopes.'
> But wherefore waste I time to counsel thee,
> That art a votary to fond desire?
> Once more adieu! my father at the road
> Expects my coming, there to see me shipp'd.

**From *The Two Gentlemen of Verona*,
Act One, Scene 1**

VALENTINE

Go to, sir: tell me, do you know Madam Silvia?

SPEED

She that your worship loves?

VALENTINE

Why, how know you that I am in love?

SPEED

Marry, by these special marks: first, you have learned, like Sir Proteus, to wreathe your arms, like a malcontent; to relish a love-song, like a robin-redbreast; to walk alone, like one that had the pestilence; to sigh, like a school-boy that had lost his ABC; to weep, like a young wench that had buried her grandam; to fast, like one that takes diet; to watch like one that fears robbing; to speak puling, like a beggar at Hallowmas. You were wont, when you laughed, to crow like a cock; when you walked, to walk like one of the lions; when you fasted, it was presently after dinner; when you looked sadly, it was for want of money: and now you are metamorphosed with a mistress, that, when I look on you, I can hardly think you my master.

VALENTINE

Are all these things perceived in me?

SPEED

They are all perceived without ye.

VALENTINE

Without me? they cannot.

SPEED

Without you? nay, that's certain, for, without you were so simple, none else would: but you are so without these follies, that these follies are within you and shine through you like the water in an urinal, that not an eye that sees you but is a physician to comment on your malady.

VALENTINE

But tell me, dost thou know my lady Silvia?

SPEED

She that you gaze on so as she sits at supper?

VALENTINE

Hast thou observed that? even she, I mean.

SPEED

Why, sir, I know her not.

VALENTINE

Dost thou know her by my gazing on her, and
yet knowest her not?

SPEED

Is she not hard-favoured, sir?

VALENTINE

Not so fair, boy, as well-favoured.

SPEED

Sir, I know that well enough.

VALENTINE

What dost thou know?

SPEED

That she is not so fair as, of you, well-
favoured.

VALENTINE

I mean that her beauty is exquisite, but her
favour infinite.

SPEED

That's because the one is painted and the other
out of all count.

VALENTINE

How painted? and how out of count?

SPEED

Marry, sir, so painted, to make her fair, that no
man counts of her beauty.

VALENTINE

How esteemest thou me? I account of her
beauty.

SPEED

You never saw her since she was deformed.

VALENTINE

How long hath she been deformed?

SPEED

Ever since you loved her.

VALENTINE

I have loved her ever since I saw her; and still
I see her beautiful.

SPEED

If you love her, you cannot see her.

VALENTINE

Why?

SPEED

Because Love is blind. O, that you had mine
eyes; or your own eyes had the lights they were
wont to have when you chid at Sir Proteus for
going ungartered!

VALENTINE

What should I see then?

SPEED

Your own present folly and her passing defor-
mity: for he, being in love, could not see to
garter his hose, and you, being in love, cannot
see to put on your hose.

VALENTINE

Belike, boy, then, you are in love; for last
morning you could not see to wipe my shoes.

SPEED

True, sir; I was in love with my bed: I thank
you, you swinged me for my love, which makes
me the bolder to chide you for yours.

VALENTINE

In conclusion, I stand affected to her.

**From *The Two Gentemen of Verona*,
Act Two, scene 1**

PETRUCHIO

I pray you do. I will attend her here,
And woo her with some spirit when she comes.
Say that she rail; why then I'll tell her plain
She sings as sweetly as a nightingale:
Say that she frown, I'll say she looks as clear
As morning roses newly wash'd with dew:
Say she be mute and will not speak a word;
Then I'll commend her volubility,
And say she uttereth piercing eloquence:
If she do bid me pack, I'll give her thanks,
As though she bid me stay by her a week:
If she deny to wed, I'll crave the day
When I shall ask the banns and when be
        marrièd.
But here she comes; and now, Petruchio, speak.
    [*Enter Katharina*]
Good morrow, Kate; for that's your name, I hear.

KATHARINA

Well have you heard, but something hard of hearing:
They call me Katharina that do talk of me.

PETRUCHIO

You lie, in faith; for you are call'd plain Kate,
And bonny Kate and sometimes Kate the curst;
But Kate, the prettiest Kate in Christendom
Kate of Kate Hall, my super-dainty Kate,
For dainties are all Kates, and therefore, Kate,
Take this of me, Kate of my consolation;
Hearing thy mildness praised in every town,
Thy virtues spoke of, and thy beauty sounded,
Yet not so deeply as to thee belongs,
Myself am moved to woo thee for my wife.

KATHARINA

Moved! in good time: let him that moved you hither
Remove you hence: I knew you at the first
You were a moveable.

PETRUCHIO

                    Why, what's a moveable?

KATHARINA
A join'd-stool.
PETRUCHIO
     Thou hast hit it: come, sit on me.
KATHARINA
Asses are made to bear, and so are you.
PETRUCHIO
Women are made to bear, and so are you.
KATHARINA
No such jade as you, if me you mean.
PETRUCHIO
Alas! good Kate, I will not burden thee;
For, knowing thee to be but young and light—
KATHARINA
Too light for such a swain as you to catch;
And yet as heavy as my weight should be.
PETRUCHIO
Should be! should—buzz!
KATHARINA
Well ta'en, and like a buzzard.
PETRUCHIO
O slow-wing'd turtle! shall a buzzard take thee?
KATHARINA
Ay, for a turtle, as he takes a buzzard.
PETRUCHIO
Come, come, you wasp; i' faith, you are too angry.
KATHARINA
If I be waspish, best beware my sting.
PETRUCHIO
My remedy is then, to pluck it out.
KATHARINA
Ay, if the fool could find it where it lies,
PETRUCHIO
Who knows not where a wasp does wear his sting?
In his tail.
KATHARINA
   In his tongue.
PETRUCHIO
     Whose tongue?

KATHARINA
Yours, if you talk of tails: and so farewell.
PETRUCHIO
What, with my tongue in your tail? nay, come again,
Good Kate; I am a gentleman.
KATHARINA
That I'll try.
[She strikes him]
PETRUCHIO
I swear I'll cuff you, if you strike again.
KATHARINA
So may you lose your arms:
If you strike me, you are no gentleman;
And if no gentleman, why then no arms.
PETRUCHIO
A herald, Kate? O, put me in thy books!
KATHARINA
What is your crest? a coxcomb?
PETRUCHIO
A combless cock, so Kate will be my hen.
KATHARINA
No cock of mine; you crow too like a craven.
PETRUCHIO
Nay, come, Kate, come; you must not look so sour.
KATHARINA
It is my fashion, when I see a crab.
PETRUCHIO
Why, here's no crab; and therefore look not sour.
KATHARINA
There is, there is.
PETRUCHIO
Then show it me.
KATHARINA
Had I a glass, I would.
PETRUCHIO
What, you mean my face?
KATHARINA
Well aim'd of such a young one.
PETRUCHIO
Now, by Saint George, I am too young for you.

Katharina
Yet you are wither'd.

Petruchio
'Tis with cares.

Katharina
I care not.

Petruchio
Nay, hear you, Kate: in sooth you scape not so.

Katharina
I chafe you, if I tarry: let me go.

Petruchio
No, not a whit: I find you passing gentle.
'Twas told me you were rough and coy and sullen,
And now I find report a very liar;
For thou are pleasant, gamesome, passing
      courteous,
But slow in speech, yet sweet as spring-time
      flowers:
Thou canst not frown, thou canst not look askance,
Nor bite the lip, as angry wenches will,
Nor hast thou pleasure to be cross in talk,
But thou with mildness entertain'st thy wooers,
With gentle conference, soft and affable.
Why does the world report that Kate doth limp?
O slanderous world! Kate like the hazel-twig
Is straight and slender and as brown in hue
As hazel nuts and sweeter than the kernels.
O, let me see thee walk: thou dost not halt.

Katharina
Go, fool, and whom thou keep'st command.

Petruchio
Did ever Dian so become a grove
As Kate this chamber with her princely gait?
O, be thou Dian, and let her be Kate;
And then let Kate be chaste and Dian sportful!

Katharina
Where did you study all this goodly speech?

Petruchio
It is extempore, from my mother-wit.

Katharina
A witty mother! witless else her son.

PETRUCHIO
Am I not wise?
KATHARINA
Yes; keep you warm.
PETRUCHIO
Marry, so I mean, sweet Katharina, in thy bed:
And therefore, setting all this chat aside,
Thus in plain terms: your father hath consented
That you shall be my wife; your dowry 'greed on;
And, Will you, nill you, I will marry you.
Now, Kate, I am a husband for your turn;
For, by this light, whereby I see thy beauty,
Thy beauty, that doth make me like thee well,
Thou must be married to no man but me;
For I am he am born to tame you Kate,
And bring you from a wild Kate to a Kate
Conformable as other household Kates.
Here comes your father: never make denial;
I must and will have Katharina to my wife.
[*Re-enter Baptista, Gremio, and Tranio*]
BAPTISTA
Now, Signior Petruchio, how speed you with
my daughter?
PETRUCHIO
How but well, sir? how but well?
It were impossible I should speed amiss.
BAPTISTA
Why, how now, daughter Katharina! in your
dumps?
KATHARINA
Call you me daughter? now, I promise you
You have show'd a tender fatherly regard,
To wish me wed to one half-lunatic;
A madcap ruffian and a swearing Jack,
That thinks with oaths to face the matter out.
PETRUCHIO
Father, 'tis thus: yourself and all the world,
That talk'd of her, have talk'd amiss of her:

If she be curst, it is for policy,
For she's not froward, but modest as the dove;
She is not hot, but temperate as the morn;
For patience she will prove a second Grissel,
And Roman Lucrece for her chastity:
And to conclude, we have 'greed so well together,
That upon Sunday is the wedding-day.

KATHARINA

I'll see thee hang'd on Sunday first.

> **From *The Taming of the Shrew*,**
> **Act Two, scene 1**

KATHARINA

Husband, let's follow, to see the end of this ado.

PETRUCHIO

First kiss me, Kate, and we will.

KATHARINA

What, in the midst of the street?

PETRUCHIO

What, art thou ashamed of me?

KATHARINA

No, sir, God forbid; but ashamed to kiss.

PETRUCHIO

Why, then let's home again. Come, sirrah, let's away.

KATHARINA

Nay, I will give thee a kiss: now pray thee,
love, stay.

PETRUCHIO

Is not this well? Come, my sweet Kate:
Better once than never, for never too late.

> **From *The Taming of the Shrew*,**
> **Act Five, scene 1**

PETRUCHIO

> Katharina, I charge thee, tell these headstrong
>> women
> What duty they do owe their lords and husbands.

WIDOW

> Come, come, you're mocking: we will have no
>> telling.

PETRUCHIO

> Come on, I say; and first begin with her.

WIDOW

> She shall not.

PETRUCHIO

> I say she shall: and first begin with her.

KATHARINA

> Fie, fie! unknit that threatening unkind brow,
> And dart not scornful glances from those eyes,
> To wound thy lord, thy king, thy governor:
> It blots thy beauty as frosts do bite the meads,
> Confounds thy fame as whirlwinds shake fair buds,
> And in no sense is meet or amiable.
> A woman moved is like a fountain troubled,
> Muddy, ill-seeming, thick, bereft of beauty;
> And while it is so, none so dry or thirsty
> Will deign to sip or touch one drop of it.
> Thy husband is thy lord, thy life, thy keeper,
> Thy head, thy sovereign; one that cares for thee,
> And for thy maintenance commits his body
> To painful labour both by sea and land,
> To watch the night in storms, the day in cold,
> Whilst thou liest warm at home, secure and safe;
> And craves no other tribute at thy hands
> But love, fair looks and true obedience;
> Too little payment for so great a debt.
> Such duty as the subject owes the prince
> Even such a woman oweth to her husband;
> And when she is froward, peevish, sullen, sour,
> And not obedient to his honest will,
> What is she but a foul contending rebel
> And graceless traitor to her loving lord?

I am ashamed that women are so simple
To offer war where they should kneel for peace;
Or seek for rule, supremacy and sway,
When they are bound to serve, love and obey.
Why are our bodies soft and weak and smooth,
Unapt to toil and trouble in the world,
But that our soft conditions and our hearts
Should well agree with our external parts?
Come, come, you froward and unable worms!
My mind hath been as big as one of yours,
My heart as great, my reason haply more,
To bandy word for word and frown for frown;
But now I see our lances are but straws,
Our strength as weak, our weakness past compare,
That seeming to be most which we indeed least are.
Then vail your stomachs, for it is no boot,
And place your hands below your husband's foot:
In token of which duty, if he please,
My hand is ready; may it do him ease.

PETRUCHIO
    Why, there's a wench! Come on, and kiss me, Kate.

**From *The Taming of the Shrew*,
Act Five, scene 2**

[*Enter gentlemen, bearing the corpse of King
Henry the Sixth in an open coffin, with halberds
to guard it; Lady Anne being the mourner*]

LADY ANNE

    Set down, set down your honourable load,
    If honour may be shrouded in a hearse,
    Whilst I awhile obsequiously lament
    The untimely fall of virtuous Lancaster.
    Poor key-cold figure of a holy king!
    Pale ashes of the house of Lancaster!
    Thou bloodless remnant of that royal blood!
    Be it lawful that I invocate thy ghost,
    To hear the lamentations of Poor Anne,
    Wife to thy Edward, to thy slaughter'd son,
    Stabb'd by the selfsame hand that made these
        wounds!
    Lo, in these windows that let forth thy life,
    I pour the helpless balm of my poor eyes.
    Cursèd be the hand that made these fatal holes!
    Cursèd be the heart that had the heart to do it!
    Cursèd the blood that let this blood from hence!
    More direful hap betide that hated wretch,
    That makes us wretched by the death of thee,
    Than I can wish to adders, spiders, toads,
    Or any creeping venom'd thing that lives!
    If ever he have child, abortive be it,
    Prodigious, and untimely brought to light,
    Whose ugly and unnatural aspect
    May fright the hopeful mother at the view;
    And that be heir to his unhappiness!
    If ever he have wife, let her he made
    A miserable by the death of him
    As I am made by my poor lord and thee!
    Come, now towards Chertsey with your holy load,
    Taken from Paul's to be interrèd there;
    And still, as you are weary of the weight,
    Rest you, whiles I lament King Henry's corse.

RICHARD GLOUCESTER

Stay, you that bear the corse, and set it down.

LADY ANNE

What black magician conjures up this fiend,
To stop devoted charitable deeds?

RICHARD GLOUCESTER

Villains, set down the corse; or, by Saint Paul,
I'll make a corse of him that disobeys.

GENTLEMAN

My lord, stand back, and let the coffin pass.

RICHARD GLOUCESTER

Unmanner'd dog! stand thou, when I command:
Advance thy halbert higher than my breast,
Or, by Saint Paul, I'll strike thee to my foot,
And spurn upon thee, beggar, for thy boldness.

LADY ANNE

What, do you tremble? are you all afraid?
Alas, I blame you not; for you are mortal,
And mortal eyes cannot endure the devil.
Avaunt, thou dreadful minister of hell!
Thou hadst but power over his mortal body,
His soul thou canst not have; therefore be gone.

RICHARD GLOUCESTER

Sweet saint, for charity, be not so curst.

LADY ANNE

Foul devil, for God's sake, hence, and trouble
us not;
For thou hast made the happy earth thy hell,
Fill'd it with cursing cries and deep exclaims.
If thou delight to view thy heinous deeds,
Behold this pattern of thy butcheries.
O, gentlemen, see, see! dead Henry's wounds
Open their congeal'd mouths and bleed afresh!
Blush, blush, thou lump of foul deformity;
For 'tis thy presence that exhales this blood
From cold and empty veins, where no blood dwells;
Thy deed, inhuman and unnatural,
Provokes this deluge most unnatural.

O God, which this blood madest, revenge his death!
O earth, which this blood drink'st revenge his death!
Either heaven with lightning strike the murderer
    dead,
Or earth, gape open wide and eat him quick,
As thou dost swallow up this good king's blood
Which his hell-govern'd arm hath butcherèd!

RICHARD GLOUCESTER

Lady, you know no rules of charity,
Which renders good for bad, blessings for curses.

LADY ANNE

Villain, thou know'st no law of God nor man:
No beast so fierce but knows some touch of pity.

RICHARD GLOUCESTER

But I know none, and therefore am no beast.

LADY ANNE

O wonderful, when devils tell the truth!

RICHARD GLOUCESTER

More wonderful, when angels are so angry.
Vouchsafe, divine perfection of a woman,
Of these supposed-evils, to give me leave,
By circumstance, but to acquit myself.

LADY ANNE

Vouchsafe, diffused infection of a man,
For these known evils, but to give me leave,
By circumstance, to curse thy cursèd self.

RICHARD GLOUCESTER

Fairer than tongue can name thee, let me have
Some patient leisure to excuse myself.

LADY ANNE

Fouler than heart can think thee, thou canst make
No excuse current, but to hang thyself.

RICHARD GLOUCESTER

By such despair, I should accuse myself.

LADY ANNE

And, by despairing, shouldst thou stand excused;
For doing worthy vengeance on thyself,
Which didst unworthy slaughter upon others.

RICHARD GLOUCESTER
Say that I slew them not?
LADY ANNE
Why, then they are not dead:
But dead they are, and devilish slave, by thee.
RICHARD GLOUCESTER
I did not kill your husband.
LADY ANNE
Why, then he is alive.
RICHARD GLOUCESTER
Nay, he is dead; and slain by Edward's hand.
LADY ANNE
In thy foul throat thou liest: Queen Margaret saw
Thy murderous falchion smoking in his blood;
The which thou once didst bend against her breast,
But that thy brothers beat aside the point.
RICHARD GLOUCESTER
I was provokèd by her slanderous tongue,
That laid their guilt upon my guiltless shoulders.
LADY ANNE
Thou wast provokèd by thy bloody mind.
Which never dreamt on aught but butcheries:
Didst thou not kill this king?
RICHARD GLOUCESTER
I grant ye.
LADY ANNE
Dost grant me, hedgehog? then, God grant me too
Thou mayst be damnèd for that wicked deed!
O, he was gentle, mild, and virtuous!
RICHARD GLOUCESTER
The better for the King of heaven, that hath him.
LADY ANNE
He *is* in heaven, where thou shalt never come.
RICHARD GLOUCESTER
Let him thank me, that holp to send him thither;
For he was fitter for that place than earth.
LADY ANNE
And thou unfit for any place but hell.

RICHARD GLOUCESTER
Yes, one place else, if you will hear me name it.

LADY ANNE
Some dungeon.

RICHARD GLOUCESTER
Your bed-chamber.

LADY ANNE
I'll rest betide the chamber where thou liest!

RICHARD GLOUCESTER
So will it, madam till I lie with you.

LADY ANNE
I hope so.

RICHARD GLOUCESTER
I know so. But, gentle Lady Anne,
To leave this keen encounter of our wits,
And fall somewhat into a slower method,
Is not the causer of the timeless deaths
Of these Plantagenets, Henry and Edward,
As blameful as the executioner?

LADY ANNE
Thou art the cause, and most accursed effect.

RICHARD GLOUCESTER
Your beauty was the cause of that effect;
Your beauty: which did haunt me in my sleep
To undertake the death of all the world,
So I might live one hour in your sweet bosom.

LADY ANNE
If I thought that, I tell thee, homicide,
These nails should rend that beauty from my
　　　cheeks.

RICHARD GLOUCESTER
These eyes could never endure sweet beauty's wreck;
You should not blemish it, if I stood by:
As all the world is cheerèd by the sun,
So I by that; it is my day, my life.

LADY ANNE
Black night o'ershade thy day, and death thy life!

RICHARD GLOUCESTER
Curse not thyself, fair creature thou art both.

LADY ANNE
I would I were, to be revenged on thee.
RICHARD GLOUCESTER
It is a quarrel most unnatural,
To be revenged on him that loveth you.
LADY ANNE
It is a quarrel just and reasonable,
To be revenged on him that slew my husband.
RICHARD GLOUCESTER
He that bereft thee, lady, of thy husband,
Did it to help thee to a better husband.
LADY ANNE
His better doth not breathe upon the earth.
RICHARD GLOUCESTER
He lives that loves thee better than he could.
LADY ANNE
Name him.
RICHARD GLOUCESTER
Plantagenet.
LADY ANNE
Why, that was he.
RICHARD GLOUCESTER
The selfsame name, but one of better nature.
LADY ANNE
Where is he?
RICHARD GLOUCESTER
Here. Why dost thou spit at me?
LADY ANNE
Would it were mortal poison, for thy sake!
RICHARD GLOUCESTER
Never came poison from so sweet a place.
LADY ANNE
Never hung poison on a fouler toad.
Out of my sight! thou dost infect my eyes.
RICHARD GLOUCESTER
Thine eyes, sweet lady, have infected mine.
LADY ANNE
Would they were basilisks, to strike thee dead!

Richard Gloucester

I would they were, that I might die at once;
For now they kill me with a living death.
Those eyes of thine from mine have drawn salt
tears,
Shamed their aspect with store of childish drops:
These eyes that never shed remorseful tear,
No, when my father York and Edward wept,
To hear the piteous moan that Rutland made
When black-faced Clifford shook his sword at him;
Nor when thy warlike father, like a child,
Told the sad story of my father's death,
And twenty times made pause to sob and weep,
That all the standers-by had wet their cheeks
Like trees bedash'd with rain: in that sad time
My manly eyes did scorn an humble tear;
And what these sorrows could not thence exhale,
Thy beauty hath, and made them blind with
weeping.
I never sued to friend nor enemy;
My tongue could never learn sweet smoothing word;
But now thy beauty is proposed my fee,
My proud heart sues, and prompts my tongue
to speak.
Teach not thy lips such scorn, for they were made
For kissing, lady, not for such contempt.
If thy revengeful heart cannot forgive,
Lo, here I lend thee this sharp-pointed sword;
Which if thou please to hide in this true bosom.
And let the soul forth that adoreth thee,
I lay it naked to the deadly stroke,
And humbly beg the death upon my knee.
Nay, do not pause; for I did kill King Henry,
But 'twas thy beauty that provokèd me.
Nay, now dispatch; 'twas I that stabb'd young
Edward,
But 'twas thy heavenly face that set me on.
Take up the sword again, or take up me.

LADY ANNE

Arise, dissembler: though I wish thy death,
I will not be the executioner.

RICHARD GLOUCESTER

Then bid me kill myself, and I will do it.

LADY ANNE

I have already.

RICHARD GLOUCESTER

Tush, that was in thy rage:
Speak it again, and, even with the word,
That hand, which, for thy love, did kill thy love,
Shall, for thy love, kill a far truer love;
To both their deaths thou shalt be accessary.

LADY ANNE

I would I knew thy heart.

RICHARD GLOUCESTER

'Tis figured in my tongue.

LADY ANNE

I fear me both are false.

RICHARD GLOUCESTER

Then never man was true.

LADY ANNE

Well, well, put up your sword.

RICHARD GLOUCESTER

Say, then, my peace is made.

LADY ANNE

That shall you know hereafter.

RICHARD GLOUCESTER

But shall I live in hope?

LADY ANNE

All men, I hope, live so.

RICHARD GLOUCESTER

Vouchsafe to wear this ring.

LADY ANNE

To take is not to give.

RICHARD GLOUCESTER

Look, how this ring encompasseth finger.
Even so thy breast encloseth my poor heart;
Wear both of them, for both of them are thine.

And if thy poor devoted suppliant may
But beg one favour at thy gracious hand,
Thou dost confirm his happiness for ever.

LADY ANNE

What is it?

RICHARD GLOUCESTER

That it would please thee leave these sad designs
To him that hath more cause to be a mourner,
And presently repair to Crosby Place;
Where, after I have solemnly interr'd
At Chertsey monastery this noble king,
And wet his grave with my repentant tears,
I will with all expedient duty see you:
For divers unknown reasons. I beseech you,
Grant me this boon.

LADY ANNE

With all my heart; and much it joys me too,
To see you are become so penitent.
Tressel and Berkeley, go along with me.

RICHARD GLOUCESTER

Bid me farewell.

LADY ANNE

'Tis more than you deserve;
But since you teach me how to flatter you,
Imagine I have said farewell already.

**From *Richard III*,
Act One, scene 2**

Even as the sun with purple-colour'd face
Had ta'en his last leave of the weeping morn,
Rose-cheek'd Adonis hied him to the chase;
Hunting he loved, but love he laugh'd to scorn;
    Sick-thoughted Venus makes amain unto him,
    And like a bold-faced suitor 'gins to woo him.

'Thrice-fairer than myself,' thus she began,
'The field's chief flower, sweet above compare,
Stain to all nymphs, more lovely than a man,
More white and red than doves or roses are;
    Nature that made thee, with herself at strife,
    Saith that the world hath ending with thy life.

'Vouchsafe, thou wonder, to alight thy steed,
And rein his proud head to the saddle-bow;
If thou wilt deign this favour, for thy meed
A thousand honey secrets shalt thou know:
    Here come and sit, where never serpent hisses,
    And being set, I'll smother thee with kisses;

'And yet not cloy thy lips with loathed satiety,
But rather famish them amid their plenty,
Making them red and pale with fresh variety,
Ten kisses short as one, one long as twenty:
    A summer's day will seem an hour but short,
    Being wasted in such time-beguiling sport.'

With this she seizeth on his sweating palm,
The precedent of pith and livelihood,
And trembling in her passion, calls it balm,
Earth's sovereign salve to do a goddess good:
    Being so enraged, desire doth lend her force
    Courageously to pluck him from his horse.

Over one arm the lusty courser's rein,
Under her other was the tender boy,

Who blush'd and pouted in a dull disdain,
With leaden appetite, unapt to toy;
    She red and hot as coals of glowing fire,
    He red for shame, but frosty in desire.

The studded bridle on a ragged bough
Nimbly she fastens:—O, how quick is love!—
The steed is stallèd up, and even now
To tie the rider she begins to prove:
    Backward she push'd him, as she would be
        thrust,
    And govern'd him in strength, though not in lust.

So soon was she along as he was down,
Each leaning on their elbows and their hips:
Now doth she stroke his cheek, now doth he frown,
And 'gins to chide, but soon she stops his lips;
    And kissing speaks, with lustful language
        broken,
    'If thou wilt chide, thy lips shall never open.'

He burns with bashful shame: she with her tears
Doth quench the maiden burning of his cheeks;
Then with her windy sighs and golden hairs
To fan and blow them dry again she seeks:
    He saith she is immodest, blames her 'miss;
    What follows more she murders with a kiss.

Even as an empty eagle, sharp by fast,
Tires with her beak on feathers, flesh and bone,
Shaking her wings, devouring all in haste,
Till either gorge be stuff'd or prey be gone;
    Even so she kissed his brow, his cheek, his chin,
    And where she ends she doth anew begin.

Forced to content, but never to obey,
Panting he lies and breatheth in her face;
She feedeth on the steam as on a prey,
And calls it heavenly moisture, air of grace;
    Wishing her cheeks were gardens full of flowers,
    So they were dew'd with such distilling showers.

Look, how a bird lies tangled in a net,
So fasten'd in her arms Adonis lies;
Pure shame and awed resistance made him fret,
Which bred more beauty in his angry eyes:
    Rain added to a river that is rank
    Perforce will force it overflow the bank.

Still she entreats, and prettily entreats,
For to a pretty ear she tunes her tale;
Still is he sullen, still he lours and frets,
'Twixt crimson shame and anger ashy-pale:
    Being red, she loves him best; and being white,
    Her best is better'd with a more delight.

Look how he can, she cannot choose but love;
And by her fair immortal hand she swears,
From his soft bosom never to remove,
Till he take truce with her contending tears,
    Which long have rain'd, making her cheeks
        all wet;
    And one sweet kiss shall pay this countless debt.

Upon this promise did he raise his chin,
Like a dive-dapper peering through a wave,
Who, being look'd on, ducks as quickly in;
So offers he to give what she did crave;
    But when her lips were ready for his pay,
    He winks, and turns his lips another way.

Never did passenger in summer's heat
More thirst for drink than she for this good turn.
Her help she sees, but help she cannot get;
She bathes in water, yet her fire must burn:
    'O, pity,' 'gan she cry, 'flint-hearted boy!
    'Tis but a kiss I beg; why art thou coy?

'I have been woo'd, as I entreat thee now,
Even by the stern and direful god of war,
Whose sinewy neck in battle ne'er did bow,

Who conquers where he comes in every jar;
  Yet hath he been my captive and my slave,
  And begg'd for that which thou unask'd shalt
      have.

'Over my altars hath he hung his lance,
His batter'd shield, his uncontrollèd crest,
And for my sake hath learn'd to sport and dance,
To toy, to wanton, dally, smile and jest,
  Scorning his churlish drum and ensign red,
  Making my arms his field, his tent my bed.

'Thus he that overruled I oversway'd,
Leading him prisoner in a red-rose chain:
Strong-tempered steel his stronger strength obey'd,
Yet was he servile to my coy disdain.
  O, be not proud, nor brag not of thy might,
  For mastering her that foil'd the god of fight!

'Touch but my lips with those fair lips of thine,—
Though mine be not so fair, yet are they red—
The kiss shall be thine own as well as mine.
What seest thou in the ground? hold up thy head:
  Look in mine eye-balls, there thy beauty lies;
  Then why not lips on lips, since eyes in eyes?

'Art thou ashamed to kiss? then wink again,
And I will wink; so shall the day seem night;
Love keeps his revels where they are but twain;
Be bold to play, our sport is not in sight:
  These blue-vein'd violets whereon we lean
  Never can blab, nor know not what we mean.

'The tender spring upon thy tempting lip
Shows thee unripe; yet mayst thou well be tasted:
Make use of time, let not advantage slip;
Beauty within itself should not be wasted:
  Fair flowers that are not gather'd in their prime
  Rot and consume themselves in little time.

'Were I hard-favour'd, foul, or wrinkled-old,
Ill-nurtured, crooked, churlish, harsh in voice,
O'erworn, despised, rheumatic and cold,
Thick-sighted, barren, lean and lacking juice,
   Then mightst thou pause, for then I were not
      for thee
   But having no defects, why dost abhor me?

'Thou canst not see one wrinkle in my brow;
Mine eyes are gray and bright and quick in
      turning:
My beauty as the spring doth yearly grow,
My flesh is soft and plump, my marrow burning;
   My smooth moist hand, were it with thy hand felt,
   Would in thy palm dissolve, or seem to melt.

'Bid me discourse, I will enchant thine ear,
Or, like a fairy, trip upon the green,
Or, like a nymph, with long dishevell'd hair,
Dance on the sands, and yet no footing seen:
   Love is a spirit all compact of fire,
   Not gross to sink, but light, and will aspire.

'Witness this primrose bank whereon I lie;
These forceless flowers like sturdy trees support me;
Two strengthless doves will draw me through the sky,
From morn till night, even where I list to sport me:
   Is love so light, sweet boy, and may it be
   That thou shouldst think it heavy unto thee?

'Is thine own heart to thine own face affected?
Can thy right hand seize love upon thy left?
Then woo thyself, be of thyself rejected,
Steal thine own freedom and complain on theft.
   Narcissus so himself himself forsook,
   And died to kiss his shadow in the brook.

'Torches are made to light, jewels to wear,
Dainties to taste, fresh beauty for the use,

Herbs for their smell, and sappy plants to bear:
Things growing to themselves are growth's abuse:
   Seeds spring from seeds and beauty breedeth beauty;
     Thou wast begot; to get it is thy duty.

'Upon the earth's increase why shouldst thou feed,
Unless the earth with thy increase be fed?
By law of nature thou art bound to breed,
That thine may live when thou thyself art dead;
   And so, in spite of death, thou dost survive,
   In that thy likeness still is left alive.'
   .   .   .   .

Now which way shall she turn? what shall she say?
Her words are done, her woes are more increasing;
The time is spent, her object will away,
And from her twining arms doth urge releasing.
   'Pity,' she cries, 'some favour, some remorse!'
   Away he springs and hasteth to his horse.

But, lo, from forth a copse that neighbors by,
A breeding jennet, lusty, young and proud,
Adonis' trampling courser doth espy,
And forth she rushes, snorts and neighs aloud:
   The strong-neck'd steed, being tied unto a tree,
   Breaketh his rein, and to her straight goes he.

Imperiously he leaps, he neighs, he bounds,
And now his woven girths he breaks asunder;
The bearing earth with his hard hoof he wounds,
Whose hollow womb resounds like heaven's thunder;
   The iron bit he crusheth 'tween his teeth,
   Controlling what he was controlled with.

His ears up-prick'd; his braided hanging mane
Upon his compass'd crest now stand on end;
His nostrils drink the air, and forth again,

As from a furnace, vapours doth he send:
His eye, which scornfully glisters like fire,
Shows his hot courage and his high desire.

Sometime he trots, as if he told the steps,
With gentle majesty and modest pride;
Anon he rears upright, curvets and leaps,
As who should say 'Lo, thus my strength is tried,
And this I do to captivate the eye
Of the fair breeder that is standing by.'

What recketh he his rider's angry stir,
His flattering 'Holla,' or his 'Stand, I say'?
What cares he now for curb or pricking spur?
For rich caparisons or trapping gay?
He sees his love, and nothing else he sees,
For nothing else with his proud sight agrees.

Look, when a painter would surpass the life,
In limning out a well-proportion'd steed,
His art with nature's workmanship at strife,
As if the dead the living should exceed;
So did this horse excel a common one
In shape, in courage, colour, pace and bone.

Round-hoof'd, short-jointed, fetlocks shag and long,
Broad breast, full eye, small head and nostril wide,
High crest, short ears, straight legs and passing
         strong,
Thin mane, thick tail, broad buttock, tender hide:
Look, what a horse should have he did not lack,
Save a proud rider on so proud a back.

Sometime he scuds far off and there he stares;
Anon he starts at stirring of a feather;
To bid the wind a base he now prepares,
And whether he run or fly they know not whether;
For through his mane and tail the high wind
         sings,
Fanning the hairs, who wave like feather'd wings.

He looks upon his love and neighs unto her;
She answers him as if she knew his mind:
Being proud, as females are, to see him woo her,
She puts on outward strangeness, seems unkind,
    Spurns at his love and scorns the heat he feels,
    Beating his kind embracements with her heels.

Then, like a melancholy malcontent,
He veils his tail that, like a falling plume,
Cool shadow to his melting buttock lent:
He stamps and bites the poor flies in his fume.
    His love, perceiving how he is enraged,
    Grew kinder, and his fury was assuaged.

His testy master goeth about to take him;
When, lo, the unback'd breeder, full of fear,
Jealous of catching, swiftly doth forsake him,
With her the horse, and left Adonis there:
    As they were mad, unto the wood they hie
        them,
    Out-stripping crows that strive to over-fly them.
        .   .   .   .

Once more the engine of her thoughts began:
'O fairest mover on this mortal round,
Would thou wert as I am, and I a man,
My heart all whole as thine, thy heart my wound;
    For one sweet look thy help I would assure thee,
    Though nothing but my body's bane would cure
        thee!'

'Give me my hand,' saith he, 'why dost thou feel it?'
'Give me my heart,' saith she, 'and thou shalt
        have it:
O, give it me, lest thy hard heart do steel it,
And being steel'd, soft sighs can never grave it:
    Then love's deep groans I never shall regard,
    Because Adonis' heart hath made mine hard.'

'For shame,' he cries, 'let go, and let me go;
My day's delight is past, my horse is gone,
And 'tis your fault I am bereft him so:
I pray you hence, and leave me here alone;
    For all my mind, my thought, my busy care,
    Is how to get my palfrey from the mare.'

Thus she replies: 'Thy palfrey, as he should,
Welcomes the warm approach of sweet desire:
Affection is a coal that must be cool'd;
Else, suffer'd, it will set the heart on fire:
    The sea hath bounds, but deep desire hath none;
    Therefore no marvel though thy horse be gone.

'How like a jade he stood, tied to the tree,
Servilely master'd with a leathern rein!
But when he saw his love, his youth's fair fee,
He held such petty bondage in disdain;
    Throwing the base thong from his bending crest,
    Enfranchising his mouth, his back, his
        breast.

'Who sees his true-love in her naked bed,
Teaching the sheets a whiter hue than white,
But, when his glutton eye so full hath fed,
His other agents aim at like delight?
    Who is so faint, that dare not be so bold
    To touch the fire, the weather being cold?

'Let me excuse thy courser, gentle boy;
And learn of him, I heartily beseech thee,
To take advantage on presented joy;
Though I were dumb, yet his proceedings teach thee;
    O, learn to love; the lesson is but plain,
    And once made perfect, never lost again.'

'I know not love,' quoth he, 'nor will not know it,
Unless it be a boar, and then I chase it;
'Tis much to borrow, and I will not owe it;

My love to love is love but to disgrace it;
    For I have heard it is a life in death,
    That laughs and weeps, and all but with a
        breath.

'Who wears a garment shapeless and unfinish'd?
Who plucks the bud before one leaf put forth?
If springing things be any jot diminish'd,
They wither in their prime, prove nothing worth:
    The colt that's back'd and burden'd being young
    Loseth his pride and never waxeth strong.

'You hurt my hand with wringing; let us part,
And leave this idle theme, this bootless chat:
Remove your siege from my unyielding heart;
To love's alarms it will not ope the gate:
    Dismiss your vows, your feigned tears, your
        flattery;
    For where a heart is hard they make no battery.'

'What! canst thou talk?' quoth she, 'hast thou a
        tongue?
O, would thou hadst not, or I had no hearing!
Thy mermaid's voice hath done me double wrong;
I had my load before, now press'd with bearing:
    Melodious discord, heavenly tune harsh
        sounding,
    Ear's deep-sweet music, and heart's deep-sore
        wounding.

'Had I no eyes but ears, my ears would love
That inward beauty and invisible;
Or were I deaf, thy outward parts would move
Each part in me that were but sensible:
    Though neither eyes nor ears, to hear nor see,
    Yet should I be in love by touching thee.

'Say, that the sense of feeling were bereft me,
And that I could not see, nor hear, nor touch,
And nothing but the very smell were left me,

Yet would my love to thee be still as much;
　　For from the stillitory of thy face excelling
　　Comes breath perfumed that breedeth love by
　　　　smelling.

'But, O, what banquet wert thou to the taste,
Being nurse and feeder of the other four!
Would they not wish the feast might ever last,
And bid Suspicion double-lock the door,
　　Lest Jealousy, that sour unwelcome guest,
　　Should, by his stealing in, disturb the feast?'
　　.　　.　　.　　.　　.　　.　　.　　.　　.　　.

'Pure lips, sweet seals in my soft lips imprinted,
What bargains may I make, still to be sealing?
To sell myself I can be well contented,
So thou wilt buy and pay and use good dealing;
　　Which purchase if thou make, for fear of slips
　　Set thy seal-manual on my wax-red lips.

'A thousand kisses buys my heart from me;
And pay them at thy leisure, one by one.
What is ten hundred touches unto thee?
Are they not quickly told and quickly gone?
　　Say, for non-payment that the debt should double,
　　Is twenty hundred kisses such a trouble?

'Fair queen,' quoth he, 'if any love you owe me,
Measure my strangeness with my unripe years:
Before I know myself, seek not to know me;
No fisher but the ungrown fry forbears:
　　The mellow plum doth fall, the green sticks fast,
　　Or being early pluck'd is sour to taste.
　　.　　.　　.　　.　　.　　.　　.　　.　　.　　.

'For where Love reigns, disturbing Jealousy
Doth call himself Affection's sentinel;
Gives false alarms, suggesteth mutiny,
And in a peaceful hour doth cry "Kill, kill!"
　　Distempering gentle Love in his desire,
　　As air and water do abate the fire.

'This sour informer, this bate-breeding spy,
This canker that eats up Love's tender spring,
This carry-tale, dissentious Jealousy,
That sometime true news, sometime false doth bring,
    Knocks at my heat and whispers in mine ear
    That if I love thee, I thy death should fear:

'And more than so, presenteth to mine eye
The picture of an angry-chafing boar,
Under whose sharp fangs on his back doth lie
An image like thyself, all stain'd with gore;
    Whose blood upon the fresh flowers being shed
    Doth make them droop with grief and hang
        the head.

'What should I do, seeing thee so indeed,
That tremble at the imagination?
The thought of it doth make my faint heart bleed,
And fear doth teach it divination:
    I prophesy thy death, my living sorrow,
    If thou encounter with the boar to-morrow.
        .   .   .   .

'If love have lent you twenty thousand tongues,
And every tongue more moving than your own,
Bewitching like the wanton mermaid's songs,
Yet from mine ear the tempting tune is blown
    For know, my heart stands armèd in mine ear,
    And will not let a false sound enter there;

'Lest the deceiving harmony should run
Into the quiet closure of my breast;
And then my little heart were quite undone,
In his bedchamber to be barr'd of rest.
    No, lady, no; my heart longs not to groan,
    But soundly sleeps, while now it sleeps alone.

'What have you urged that I cannot reprove?
The path is smooth that leadeth on to danger:
I hate not love, but your device in love,
That lends embracements unto every stranger.

You do it for increase: O strange excuse,
When reason is the bawd to lust's abuse!

'Call it not love, for Love to heaven is fled,
Since sweating Lust on earth usurp'd his name;
Under whose simple semblance he hath fed
Upon fresh beauty, blotting it with blame;
    Which the hot tyrant stains and soon bereaves,
    As caterpillars do the tender leaves.

'Love comforteth like sunshine after rain,
But Lust's effect is tempest after sun;
Love's gentle spring doth always fresh remain,
Lust's winter comes ere summer half be done;
    Love surfeits not, Lust like a glutton dies;
    Love is all truth, Lust full of forgèd lies.

'More I could tell, but more I dare not say;
The text is old, the orator too green.
Therefore, in sadness, now I will away;
My face is full of shame, my heart of teen:
    Mine ears, that to your wanton talk attended,
    Do burn themselves for having so offended.'

   .   .   .   .

'Hard-favour'd tyrant, ugly, meagre, lean,
Hateful divorce of love,'—thus chides she Death,—
'Grim-grinning ghost, earth's worm, what dost
    thou mean
To stifle beauty and to steal his breath,
    Who when he lived, his breath and beauty set
    Gloss on the rose, smell to the violet?

'If he be dead,—O no, it cannot be,   .
Seeing his beauty, thou shouldst strike at it:—
O yes, it may; thou hast no eyes to see,
But hatefully at random dost thou hit.
    Thy mark is feeble age, but thy false dart
    Mistakes that aim and cleaves an infant's heart.

'Hadst thou but bid beware, then he had spoke,
And, hearing him, thy power had lost his power.
The Destinies will curse thee for this stroke;
They bid thee crop a weed, thou pluck'st a flower:
    Love's golden arrow at him should have fled,
    And not Death's ebon dart, to strike dead.

'Dost thou drink tears, that thou provokest such
        weeping?
What may a heavy groan advantage thee?
Why hast thou cast into eternal sleeping
Those eyes that taught all other eyes to see?
    Now Nature cares not for thy mortal vigour,
    Since her best work is ruin'd with thy rigour.'
        .   .   .   .

'My tongue cannot express my grief for one,
And yet,' quoth she, 'behold two Adons dead!
My sighs are blown away, my salt tears gone,
Mine eyes are turn'd to fire, my heart to lead:
    Heavy heart's lead, melt at mine eyes' red fire!
    So shall I die by drops of hot desire.

'Alas, poor world, what treasure hast thou lost!
What face remains alive that's worth the viewing?
Whose tongue is music now? what canst thou
        boast
Of things long since, or any thing ensuing?
    The flowers are sweet, their colours fresh and
        trim;
    But true-sweet beauty lived and died with him.

'Bonnet nor veil henceforth no creature wear!
Nor sun nor wind will ever strive to kiss you:
Having no fair to lose, you need not fear;
The sun doth scorn you and the wind doth hiss you:
    But when Adonis lived, sun and sharp air
    Lurk'd like two thieves, to rob him of his fair:

'And therefore would he put his bonnet on,
Under whose brim the gaudy sun would peep;
The wind would blow it off and, being gone,
Play with his locks: then would Adonis weep;
    And straight, in pity of his tender years,
    They both would strive who first should dry
        his tears.

'To see his face the lion walk'd along
Behind some hedge, because he would not fear him;
To recreate himself when he hath sung,
The tiger would be tame and gently hear him;
    If he had spoke, the wolf would leave his prey
    And never fright the silly lamb that day.

'When he beheld his shadow in the brook,
The fishes spread on it their golden gills;
When he was by, the birds such pleasure took,
That some would sing, some other in their bills
    Would bring him mulberries and ripe-red cherries;
    He fed them with his sight, they him with berries.

'But this foul, grim, and urchin-snouted boar,
Whose downward eye still looketh for a grave,
Ne'er saw the beauteous livery that he wore;
Witness the entertainment that he gave:
    If he did see his face, why then I know
    He thought to kiss him, and hath kill'd him so.

''Tis true, 'tis true; thus was Adonis slain:
He ran upon the boar with his sharp spear,
Who did not whet his teeth at him again,
But by a kiss thought to persuade him there;
    And nuzzling in his flank, the loving swine
    Sheathed unaware the tusk in his soft groin.

'Had I been tooth'd like him, I must confess,
With kissing him I should have kill'd him first;

But he is dead, and never did he bless
My youth with his; the more am I accurst.'
    With this, she falleth in the place she stood,
    And stains her face with his congealèd blood.

She looks upon his lips, and they are pale;
She takes him by the hand, and that is cold;
She whispers in his ears a heavy tale,
As if they heard the woeful words she told;
    She lifts the coffer-lids that close his eyes,
    Where, lo, two lamps, burnt out, in darkness lies;

Two glasses, where herself herself beheld
A thousand times, and now no more reflect;
Their virtue lost, wherein they late excell'd,
And every beauty robb'd of his effect:
    'Wonder of time,' quoth she, 'this is my spite,
    That, thou being dead, the day should yet be light.

'Since thou art dead, lo, here I prophesy:
Sorrow on love hereafter shall attend:
It shall be waited on with jealousy,
Find sweet beginning, but unsavoury end,
    Ne'er settled equally, but high or low,
    That all love's pleasure shall not match his woe.

'It shall be fickle, false and full of fraud,
Bud and be blasted in a breathing-while;
The bottom poison, and the top o'erstraw'd
With sweets that shall the truest sight beguile:
    The strongest body shall it make most weak,
    Strike the wise dumb and teach the fool to speak.

'It shall be sparing and too full of riot,
Teaching decrepit age to tread the measures;
The staring ruffian shall it keep in quiet,
Pluck down the rich, enrich the poor with treasures;
    It shall be raging-mad and silly-mild,
    Make the young old, the old become a child.

'It shall suspect where is no cause of fear;
It shall not fear where it should most mistrust;
It shall be merciful and too severe,
And most deceiving when it seems most just;
    Perverse it shall be where it shows most toward,
    Put fear to valour, courage to the coward.

'It shall be cause of war and dire events,
And set dissension 'twixt the son and sire;
Subject and servile to all discontents,
As dry combustious matter is to fire:
    Sith in his prime Death doth my love destroy,
    They that love best their loves shall not
        enjoy.'

By this, the boy that by her side lay kill'd
Was melted like a vapour from her sight,
And in his blood that on the ground lay spill'd,
A purple flower sprung up, chequer'd with white,
    Resembling well his pale cheeks and the blood
    Which in round drops upon their whiteness
        stood.

She bows her head, the new-sprung flower to smell,
Comparing it to her Adonis' breath,
And says, within her bosom it shall dwell,
Since he himself is reft from her by death:
    She crops the stalk, and in the breach appears
    Green dropping sap, which she compares to
        tears.

'Poor flower,' quoth she, 'this was thy father's
        guise—
Sweet issue of a more sweet-smelling sire—
For every little grief to wet his eyes:
To grow unto himself was his desire,
    And so 'tis thine; but know, it is as good
    To wither in my breast as in his blood.

'Here was thy father's bed, here in my breast;
Thou art the next of blood, and 'tis thy right:
Lo, in this hollow cradle take thy rest,
My throbbing heart shall rock thee day and night:
 There shall not be one minute in an hour
 Wherein I will not kiss my sweet love's flower.'

Thus weary of the world, away she hies,
And yokes her silver doves; by whose swift aid
Their mistress mounted through the empty skies
In her light chariot quickly is convey'd;
 Holding their course to Paphos, where their queen
 Means to immure herself and not be seen.

From _Venus and Adonis_

LUCIANA

And may it be that you have quite forgot
    A husband's office? shall, Antipholus.
Even in the spring of love, thy love-springs rot?
    Shall love, in building, grow so ruinous?
If you did wed my sister for her wealth,
    Then for her wealth's sake use her with
        more kindness:
Or if you like elsewhere, do it by stealth;
    Muffle your false love with some show of
        blindness:
Let not my sister read it in your eye;
    Be not thy tongue thy own shame's orator;
Look sweet, be fair, become disloyalty;
    Apparel vice like virtue's harbinger;
Bear a fair presence, though your heart be tainted;
    Teach sin the carriage of a holy saint;
Be secret-false: what need she be acquainted?
    What simple thief brags of his own attaint?
'Tis double wrong, to truant with your bed
    And let her read it in thy looks at board:
Shame hath a bastard fame, well managed;
    Ill deeds are doubled with an evil word.
Alas, poor women! make us but believe,
    Being compact of credit, that you love us;
Though others have the arm, show us the sleeve;
    We in your motion turn and you may move us.
Then, gentle brother, get you in again;
    Comfort my sister, cheer her, call her wife:
'Tis holy sport to be a little vain,
    When the sweet breath of flattery conquers
        strife

ANTIPHOLUS OF SYRACUSE

Sweet mistress—what your name is else, I
    know not,
    Nor by what wonder you do hit of mine,—
Less in your knowledge and your grace you
    show not
    Than our earth's wonder, more than earth
        divine.

Teach me, dear creature, how to think and speak;
  Lay open to my earthy-gross conceit,
Smother'd in errors, feeble, shallow, weak,
  The folded meaning of your words' deceit.
Against my soul's pure truth why labour you
  To make it wander in an unknown field?
Are you a god? would you create me new?
  Transform me then, and to your power I'll
    yield.
But if that I am I, then well I know
  Your weeping sister is no wife of mine,
Nor to her bed no homage do I owe
  Far more, far more to you do I decline.
O, train me not, sweet mermaid, with thy note,
  To drown me in thy sister's flood of tears:
Sing, siren, for thyself and I will dote:
  Spread o'er the silver waves thy golden hairs,
And as a bed I'll take them and there lie,
  And in that glorious supposition think
He gains by death that hath such means to die:
  Let Love, being light, be drowned if she sink!

LUCIANA

What, are you mad, that you do reason so?

ANTIPHOLUS OF SYRACUSE

Not mad, but mated; how, I do not know.

LUCIANA

It is a fault that springeth from your eye.

ANTIPHOLUS OF SYRACUSE

For gazing on your beams, fair sun, being by.

LUCIANA

Gaze where you should, and that will clear
    your sight.

ANTIPHOLUS OF SYRACUSE

As good to wink, sweet love, as look on night.

LUCIANA

Why call you me 'love'? call my sister so.

ANTIPHOLUS OF SYRACUSE

Thy sister's sister.

LUCIANA

                That's my sister.

ANTIPHOLUS OF SYRACUSE

No;
It is thyself, mine own self's better part,
Mine eye's clear eye, my dear heart's dearer heart,
My food, my fortune and my sweet hope's aim,
My sole earth's heaven and my heaven's claim.

LUCIANA

All this my sister is, or else should be.

ANTIPHOLUS OF SYRACUSE

Call thyself sister, sweet, for I am thee.
Thee will I love and with thee lead my life:
Thou hast no husband yet nor I no wife.
Give me thy hand.

LUCIANA

O, soft, air! hold you still:
I'll fetch my sister, to get her good will.

**From *The Comedy of Errors*,
Act Three, scene 2**

ARMADO

I will hereupon confess I am in love; and as it is base for a soldier to love, so am I in love with a base wench. If drawing my sword against the humour of affection would deliver me from the reprobate thought of it, I would take desire prisoner and ransom him to any French courtier for a new-devised curtsy. I think scorn to sigh. Methinks I should outswear Cupid. Comfort me, boy. What great men have been in love?

MOTE

Hercules, master.

ARMADO

Most sweet Hercules! More authority, dear boy. Name more—and, sweet my child, let them be men of good repute and carriage.

MOTE

Samson, master; he was a man of good carriage, great carriage, for he carried the town-gates on his back like a porter, and he was in love.

ARMADO

O well-knit Samson, strong jointed Samson! I do excel thee in my rapier as much as thou didst me in carrying gates. I am in love, too. Who was Samson's love, my dear Mote?

MOTE

A woman, master.

ARMADO

Of what complexion?

MOTE

Of all the four, or the three, or the two, or one of the four.

ARMADO

Tell me precisely of what complexion?

MOTE

Of the sea-water green, sir.

ARMADO

Is that one of the four complexions?

MOTE

As I have read, sir; and the best of them, too.

ARMADO

Green indeed is the colour of lovers, but to have a love of that colour, methinks Samson had small reason for it. He surely affected her for her wit.

MOTE

It was so, sir, for she had a green wit.

ARMADO

My love is most immaculate white and red.

MOTE

Most maculate thoughts, master, are masked under such colours.

ARMADO

Define, define, well-educated infant.

MOTE

My father's wit and my mother's tongue assist me!

ARMADO

Sweet invocation of a child!—most pretty and pathetical.

MOTE

> If she be made of white and red
>> Her faults will ne'er be known,
> For blushing cheeks by faults are bred
>> And fears by pale white shown.
> Then if she fear or be to blame,
>> By this you shall not know
> For still her cheeks possess the same
>> Which native she doth owe.

A dangerous rhyme, master, against the reason of white and red.

. . . .

ARMADO

I do affect the very ground—which is base—where her shoe—which is baser—guided by her foot—which is basest—doth tread. I shall be forsworn—which is a great argument of falsehood—if I love. And how can that be true love which is falsely attempted? Love is a familiar; love is a devil. There is no evil angel but love. Yet was Samson so tempted, and he had an excellent strength. Yet was Solomon so seduced, and he had a very good wit. Cupid's butt-shaft is too hard for Hercules' club, and therefore too much odds for a Spaniard's rapier. The first and second cause will not serve my turn: the passado he respects not, the duello he regards not. His disgrace is to be called boy, but his glory is to subdue men. Adieu, valour; rust, rapier; be still drum: for your manager is in love; yea, he loveth. Assist me, some extemporal god of rhyme, for I am sure I shall turn sonnet. Devise wit, write pen, for I am for whole volumes, in folio.

From *Love's Labour's Lost*,
Act One, scene 2

BIRON
    And I, forsooth, in love—I that have been
        love's whip,
    A very beadle to a humorous sigh,
    A critic, nay, a night-watch constable,
    A domineering pedant o'er the boy,
    Than whom no mortal so magnificent.
    This wimpled, whining, purblind, wayward boy,
    This Signor Junior, giant dwarf, Dan Cupid,
    Regent of love-rhymes, lord of folded arms,
    Th'anointed sovereign of sighs and groans,
    Liege of all loiterers and malcontents,

Dread prince of plackets, king of codpieces,
Sole imperator and great general
Of trotting paritors—O my little heart!
And I to be a corporal of his field,
And wear his colours like a tumbler's hoop!
What? I love, I sue, I seek a wife?—
A woman, that is like a German clock,
Still a-repairing, ever out of frame,
And never going aright, being a watch,
But being watched that it may still go right.
Nay, to be perjured, which is worst of all,
And among three to love the worst of all—
A whitely wanton with a velvet brow
With two pitch-balls stuck in her face for eyes—
Ay, and, by heaven, one that will do the deed
Though Argus were her eunuch and her guard.
And I to sigh for her, to watch for her,
To pray for her—go to, it is a plague
That Cupid will impose for my neglect
Of his almighty dreadful little might.
Well, I will love, write, sigh, pray, sue, groan:
Some men must love my lady, and some Joan.

From *Love's Labour's Lost*,
Act Three, scene 1

KING
> What, did these rent lines show some love of
>   thine?

BIRON
> 'Did they,' quoth you? Who sees the heavenly
>   Rosaline
> That, like a rude and savage man of Ind
>   At the first op'ning of the gorgeous east,
> Bows not his vassal head and, strucken blind,

Kisses the base ground with obedient breast?
What peremptory eagle-sighted eye
  Dares look upon the heaven of her brow
That is not blinded by her majesty?

KING

  What zeal, what fury hath inspired thee now?
My love, her mistress, is a gracious moon
  She an attending star, scarce seen a light.

BIRON

My eyes are then no eyes, nor I Biron.
  O, but for my love, day would turn to night.
Of all complexions the culled sovereignty
  Do meet as at a fair in her fair cheek
Where several worthies make one dignity,
    Where nothing wants that want itself doth
      seek.
Lend me the flourish of all gentle tongues—
  Fie, painted rhetoric! O, she needs it not.
To things of sale a seller's praise belongs.
    She passes praise—then praise too short
      doth blot.
A withered hermit fivescore winters worn
  Might shake off fifty, looking in her eye.
Beauty doth varnish age as if new-born
  And gives the crutch the cradle's infancy.
O, 'tis the sun that maketh all things shine.

KING

By heaven, thy love is black as ebony.

BIRON

Is ebony like her? O word divine!
  A wife of such wood were felicity.
O, who can give an oath? Where is a book,
  That I may swear beauty doth beauty lack
If that she learn not of her eye to look?
  No face is fair that is not full so black.

KING

O paradox! Black is the badge of hell,
  The hue of dungeons and the style of night
And beauty's crest becomes the heavens well.

BIRON

Devils soonest tempt, resembling spirits of light.
O, if in black my lady's brows be decked
It mourns that painting and usurping hair
Should ravish doters with a false aspect
And therefore is she born to make black fair.
Her favour turns the fashion of the days,
For native blood is counted painting now,
And therefore red that would avoid dispraise
Paints itself black to imitate her brow.

  .   .   .   .

BIRON

                     O,'tis more than need.
Have at you, then, affection's men-at-arms.
Consider what you first did swear unto:
To fast, to study, and to see no woman—
Flat treason 'gainst the kingly state of youth.
Say, can you fast? Your stomachs are too young,
And abstinence engenders maladies.
O, we have made a vow to study, lords,
And in that vow we have forsworn our books,
For when would you, my liege, or you, or you
In leaden contemplation have found out
Such fiery numbers as the prompting eyes
Of beauty's tutors have enriched you with?
Other slow arts entirely keep the brain,
And therefore, finding barren practisers,
Scarce show a harvest of their heavy toil.
But love, first learnèd in a lady's eyes,
Lives not alone immurèd in the brain,
But with the motion of all elements
Courses as swift as thought in every power,
And gives to every power a double power
Above their functions and their offices.
It adds a precious seeing to the eye—
A lover's eyes will gaze an eagle blind.
A lover's ear will hear the lowest sound
When the suspicious head of theft is stopped.

Love's feeling is more soft and sensible
Than are the tender horns of cockled snails.
Love's tongue proves dainty Bacchus gross in taste.
For valour, is not love a Hercules,
Still climbing trees in the Hesperides?
Subtle as Sphinx, as sweet and musical
As bright Apollo's lute strung with his hair;
And when love speaks, the voice of all the gods
Make heaven drowsy with the harmony.
Never durst poet touch a pen to write
Until his ink were tempered with love's sighs.
O, then his lines would ravish savage ears,
And plant in tyrants mild humility.
From women's eyes this doctrine I derive.
They sparkle still the right Promethean fire.
They are the books, the arts, the academes
That show, contain, and nourish all the world,
Else none at all in aught proves excellent.
Then fools you were these women to forswear,
Or keeping what is sworn, you will prove fools.
For wisdom's sake—a word that all men love—
Or for love's sake—a word that loves all
        men—
Or for men's sake—the authors of these
        women—
Or women's sake—by whom we men are
        men—
Let us once lose our oaths to find ourselves,
Or else we lose ourselves to keep our oaths.
It is religion to be thus forsworn,
For charity itself fulfils the law,
And who can sever love from charity?

From *Love's Labour's Lost*,
Act Four, scene 3

HERMIA

If then true lovers have been ever cross'd,
It stands as an edict in destiny:
Then let us teach our trial patience,
Because it is a customary cross,
As due to love as thoughts and dreams and sighs,
Wishes and tears, poor fancy's followers.

. . . .

HELENA

How happy some o'er other some can be!
Through Athens I am thought as fair as she.
But what of that? Demetrius thinks not so;
He will not know what all but he do know:
And as he errs, doting on Hermia's eyes,
So I, admiring of his qualities:
Things base and vile, folding no quantity,
Love can transpose to form and dignity:
Love looks not with the eyes, but with the mind;
And therefore is wing'd Cupid painted blind:
Nor hath Love's mind of any judgement taste;
Wings and no eyes figure unheedy haste:
And therefore is Love said to be a child,
Because in choice he is so oft beguiled.
As waggish boys in game themselves forswear,
So the boy Love is perjured every where:
For ere Demetrius look'd on Hermia's eyne,
He hail'd down oaths that he was only mine;
And when this hail some heat from Hermia felt,
So he dissolved, and showers of oaths did melt.
I will go tell him of fair Hermia's flight:
Then to the wood will he to-morrow night
Pursue her; and for this intelligence
If I have thanks, it is a dear expense:
But herein mean I to enrich my pain,
To have his sight thither and back again.

**From *A Midsummer Night's Dream*,
Act One, scene 1**

DEMETRIUS

I love thee not, therefore pursue me not.
Where is Lysander and fair Hermia?
The one I'll slay, the other slayeth me.
Thou told'st me they were stolen unto this wood;
And here am I, and wood within this wood,
Because I cannot meet my Hermia.
Hence, get thee gone, and follow me no more.

HELENA

You draw me, you hard-hearted adamant;
But yet you draw not iron, for my heart
Is true as steel: leave you your power to draw,
And I shall have no power to follow you.

DEMETRIUS

Do I entice you? do I speak you fair?
Or, rather, do I not in plainest truth
Tell you, I do not, nor I cannot love you?

HELENA

And even for that do I love you the more.
I am your spaniel; and, Demetrius,
The more you beat me, I will fawn on you:
Use me but as your spaniel, spurn me, strike me,
Neglect me, lose me; only give me leave,
Unworthy as I am, to follow you.
What worser place can I beg in your love,—
And yet a place of high respect with me,—
Than to be usèd as you use your dog?

**From *A Midsummer Night's Dream*,
Act Two, scene 1**

TITANIA

    I pray thee, gentle mortal, sing again:
    Mine ear is much enamour'd of thy note;
    So is mine eye enthrallèd to thy shape;
    And thy fair virtue's force perforce doth move me
    On the first view to say, to swear, I love thee.

BOTTOM

    Methinks, mistress, you should have little reason for that: and yet, to say the truth, reason and love keep little company together now-a-days; the more the pity that some honest neighbours will not make them friends. Nay, I can gleek upon occasion.

> **From *A Midsummer Night's Dream*,**
> **Act Three, scene 2**

THESEUS

    More strange than true: I never may believe
    These antique fables, nor these fairy toys.
    Lovers and madmen have such seething brains,
    Such shaping fantasies, that apprehend
    More than cool reason ever comprehends.
    The lunatic, the lover and the poet
    Are of imagination all compact:
    One sees more devils than vast hell can hold,
    That is, the madman: the lover, all as frantic,
    Sees Helen's beauty in a brow of Egypt:
    The poet's eye, in fine frenzy rolling,
    Doth glance from heaven to earth, from earth
        to heaven;
    And as imagination bodies forth
    The forms of things unknown, the poet's pen
    Turns them to shapes and gives to airy nothing
    A local habitation and a name.
    Such tricks hath strong imagination,
    That if it would but apprehend some joy,
    It comprehends some bringer of that joy;
    Or in the night, imagining some fear,
    How easy is a bush supposed a bear!

                From *A Midsummer Night's Dream*,
                             Act Five, scene 1

ROMEO

When the devout religion of mine eye
  Maintains such falsehood, then turn tears to
    fires;
And these, who often drown'd could never die,
  Transparent heretics, be burnt for liars!
One fairer than my love! the all-seeing sun
Ne'er saw her match since first the world begun.

From *Romeo and Juliet*,
Act One, scene 2

LADY CAPULET

What say you? can you love the gentleman?
This night you shall behold him at our feast;
Read o'er the volume of young Paris' face,
And find delight writ there with beauty's pen;
Examine every married lineament,
And see how one another lends content
And what obscured in this fair volume lies
Find written in the margent of his eyes.
This precious book of love, this unbound lover,
To beautify him, only lacks a cover:
The fish lives in the sea, and 'tis much pride
For fair without the fair within to hide:
That book in many's eyes doth share the glory,
That in gold clasps locks in the golden story;
So shall you share all that he doth possess,
By having him, making yourself no less.

From *Romeo and Juliet*,
Act One, scene 3

MERCUTIO
  You are a lover; borrow Cupid's wings,
  And soar with them above a common bound.
ROMEO
  I am too sore empiercèd with his shaft
  To soar with his light feathers, and so bound,
  I cannot bound a pitch above dull woe:
  Under love's heavy burden do I sink.
MERCUTIO
  And, to sink in it, should you burden love;
  Too great oppression for a tender thing.
ROMEO
  Is love a tender thing? it is too rough,
  Too rude, too boisterous, and it pricks like thorn.
MERCUTIO
  If love be rough with you, be rough with love;
  Prick love for pricking, and you beat love down.
  Give me a case to put my visage in:
  A visor for a visor! what care I
  What curious eye doth quote deformities?
  Here are the beetle brows shall blush for me.

**From *Romeo and Juliet*,
Act One, scene 4**

ROMEO
  O, she doth teach the torches to burn bright!
  It seems she hangs upon the cheek of night
  Like a rich jewel in an Ethiope's ear;
  Beauty too rich for use, for earth too dear!
  So shows a snowy dove trooping with crows,
  As yonder lady o'er her fellows shows.
  The measure done, I'll watch her place of stand,
  And, touching hers, make blessèd my rude
      hand.

Did my heart love till now? forswear it, sight!
For I ne'er saw true beauty till this night.

. . . .

ROMEO

If I profane with my unworthiest hand
    This holy shrine, the gentler sin is this:
My lips, two blushing pilgrims, ready stand
    To smooth that rough touch with a tender kiss.

JULIET

Good pilgrim, you do wrong your hand too much,
    Which mannerly devotion shows in this;
For saints have hands that pilgrims' hands do
        touch,
And palm to palm is holy palmers' kiss.

ROMEO

Have not saints lips, and holy palmers too?

JULIET

    Ay, pilgrim, lips that they must use in prayer.

ROMEO

O, then, dear saint, let lips do what hands do;
    They pray, grant thou, lest faith turn to
        despair.

JULIET

Saints do not move, though grant for prayers' sake.

ROMEO

Then move not, while my prayer's effect I take.
Thus from my lips, by yours, my sin is purged.

JULIET

Then have my lips the sin that they have took.

ROMEO

Sin from thy lips? O trespass sweetly urged!
Give me my sin again.

JULIET

                    You kiss by the book.

**From *Romeo and Juliet*,
Act One, scene 5**

CHORUS

Now old desire doth in his death-bed lie,
  And young affection gapes to be his heir;
That fair for which love groan'd for and would die,
  With tender Juliet match'd, is now not fair.
Now Romeo is beloved and loves again,
  Alike betwitchèd by the charm of looks,
But to his foe supposed he must complain,
  And she steal love's sweet bait from fearful
    hooks:
Being held a foe, he may not have access
  To breathe such vows as lovers use to swear;
And she as much in love, her means much less
  To meet her new-belovèd any where:
But passion lends them power, time means, to meet
  Tempering extremities with extreme sweet.

  .   .   .   .

MERCUTIO

                    Nay, I'll conjure too.
Romeo! humours! madman! passion! lover!
Appear thou in the likeness of a sigh:
Speak but one rhyme, and I am satisfied;
Cry but 'Ay me!' pronounce but 'love' and 'dove';
Speak to my gossip Venus one fair word,
One nick-name for her purblind son and heir,
Young Adam Cupid, he that shot so trim,
When King Cophetua loved the beggar-maid!
He heareth not, he stirreth not, he moveth not;
The ape is dead, and I must conjure him.
I conjure thee by Rosaline's bright eyes,
By her high forehead and her scarlet lip,
By her fine foot, straight leg and quivering thigh
And the demesnes that there adjacent lie,
That in thy likeness thou appear to us!

BENVOLIO

And if he hear thee, thou wilt anger him.

MERCUTIO

This cannot anger him: 'twould anger him

To raise a spirit in his mistress' circle
Of some strange nature, letting it there stand
Till she had laid it and conjured it down;
That were some spite: my invocation
Is fair and honest, and in his mistress' name
I conjure only but to raise up him.

BENVOLIO

Come, he hath hid himself among these trees,
To be consorted with the humorous night:
Blind is his love and best befits the dark.

MERCUTIO

If love be blind, love cannot hit the mark.
Now will he sit under a medlar tree,
And wish his mistress were that kind of fruit
As maids call medlars, when they laugh alone.
Romeo, that she were, O, that she were
An open-arse, and thou a poperin pear!
Romeo, good night: I'll to my truckle-bed;
This field-bed is too cold for me to sleep:
Come, shall we go?

BENVOLIO

Go, then; for 'tis in vain
To seek him here that means not to be found.
[*Exit Benvolio and Mercutio. Enter Romeo*]

ROMEO

He jests at scars that never felt a wound.
But, soft! what light through yonder window
breaks?
It is the east, and Juliet is the sun.
Arise, fair sun, and kill the envious moon,
Who is already sick and pale with grief,
That thou her maid art far more fair than she:
Be not her maid, since she is envious;
Her vestal livery is but sick and green
And none but fools do wear it; cast it off.
It is my lady, O, it is my love!
O, that she knew she were!
She speaks yet she says nothing: what of that?
Her eye discourses; I will answer it.

I am too bold, 'tis not to me she speaks:
Two of the fairest stars in all the heaven,
Having some business, do entreat her eyes
To twinkle in their spheres till they return.
What if her eyes were there, they in her head?
The brightness of her cheek would shame
those stars,
As daylight doth a lamp; her eyes in heaven
Would through the airy region stream so bright
That birds would sing and think it were not night.
See, how she leans her cheek upon her hand!
O, that I were a glove upon that hand,
That I might touch that cheek!

JULIET

Ay me!

ROMEO

She speaks:
O, speak again, bright angel! for thou art
As glorious to this night, being o'er my head
As is a wingèd messenger of heaven
Unto the white-upturnèd wondering eyes
Of mortals that fall back to gaze on him
When he bestrides the lazy-pacing clouds
And sails upon the bosom of the air.

JULIET

O Romeo, Romeo! wherefore art thou Romeo?
Deny thy father and refuse thy name;
Or, if thou wilt not, be but sworn my love,
And I'll no longer be a Capulet.

ROMEO [Aside]

Shall I hear more, or shall I speak at this?

JULIET

'Tis but thy name that is my enemy;
Thou art thyself, though not a Montague.
What's Montague? it is nor hand, nor foot,
Nor arm, nor face, nor any other part
Belonging to a man. O, be some other name!
What's in a name? that which we call a rose

By any other name would smell as sweet;
So Romeo would, were he not Romeo call'd,
Retain that dear perfection which he owes
Without that title. Romeo, doff thy name,
And for that name which is no part of thee
Take all myself.

ROMEO

            I take thee at thy word:
Call me but love, and I'll be new baptized;
Henceforth I never will be Romeo.

JULIET

What man art thou that thus bescreen'd in night
So stumblest on my counsel?

ROMEO

                By a name
I know not how to tell thee who I am:
My name, dear saint, is hateful to myself,
Because it is an enemy to thee;
Had I it written, I would tear the word.

JULIET

My ears have not yet drunk a hundred words
Of that tongue's utterance, yet I know the sound:
Art thou not Romeo and a Montague?

ROMEO

Neither, fair saint, if either thee dislike.

JULIET

How camest thou hither, tell me, and wherefore?
The orchard walls are high and hard to climb,
And the place death, considering who thou art,
If any of my kinsmen find thee here.

ROMEO

With love's light wings did I o'er-perch these walls;
For stony limits cannot hold love out,
And what love can do that dares love attempt;
Therefore thy kinsmen are no let to me.

JULIET

If they do see thee, they will murder thee.

ROMEO

Alack, there lies more peril in thine eye

Than twenty of their swords: look thou but sweet,
And I am proof against their enmity.

JULIET

I would not for the world they saw thee here.

ROMEO

I have night's cloak to hide me from their sight;
And but thou love me, let them find me here:
My life were better ended by their hate,
Than death proroguèd, wanting of thy love.

JULIET

By whose direction found'st thou out this place?

ROMEO

By love, who first did prompt me to inquire;
He lent me counsel and I lent him eyes.
I am no pilot; yet, wert thou as far
As that vast shore wash'd with the farthest sea,
I would adventure for such merchandise.

JULIET

Thou know'st the mask of night is on my face,
Else would a maiden blush bepaint my cheek
For that which thou hast heard me speak to-night
Fain would I dwell on form, fain, fain deny
What I have spoke: but farewell compliment!
Dost thou love me? I know thou wilt say 'Ay,'
And I will take thy word: yet if thou swear'st,
Thou mayst prove false; at lovers' perjuries
Then say, Jove laughs. O gentle Romeo,
If thou dost love, pronounce it faithfully:
Or if thou think'st I am too quickly won,
I'll frown and be perverse an say thee nay,
So thou wilt woo; but else, not for the world.
In truth, fair Montague, I am too fond,
And therefore thou mayst think my 'havior light:
But trust me, gentleman, I'll prove more true
Than those that have more cunning to be strange.
I should have been more strange, I must confess,
But that thou overheard'st, ere I was ware,
My true love's passion: therefore pardon me,

And not impute this yielding to light love,
Which the dark night hath so discoverèd.

ROMEO

Lady, by yonder blessèd moon I swear
That tips with silver all these fruit-tree tops—

JULIET

O, swear not by the moon, the inconstant moon,
That monthly changes in her circled orb,
Lest that thy love prove likewise variable.

ROMEO

What shall I swear by?

JULIET

                      Do not swear at all;
Or, if thou wilt, swear by thy gracious self,
Which is the god of my idolatry,
And I'll believe thee.

ROMEO

                    If my heart's dear love—

JULIET

Well, do not swear: although I joy in thee,
I have no joy of this contract to-night:
It is too rash, too unadvised, too sudden;
Too like the lightning, which doth cease to be
Ere one can say 'It lightens.' Sweet, good night!
This bud of love, by summer's ripening breath,
May prove a beauteous flower when next we meet.
Good night, good night! as sweet repose and rest
Come to thy heart as that within my breast!

ROMEO

O, wilt thou leave me so unsatisfied?

JULIET

What satisfaction canst thou have to-night?

ROMEO

The exchange of thy love's faithful vow for mine.

JULIET

I gave thee mine before thou didst request it:
And yet I would it were to give again.

ROMEO

Wouldst thou withdraw it? for what purpose, love?

JULIET

But to be frank, and give it thee again.
And yet I wish but for the thing I have:
My bounty is as boundless as the sea,
My love as deep; the more I give to thee,
The more I have, for both are infinite.
I hear some noise within; dear love, adieu!
Anon, good nurse! Sweet Montague, be true.
Stay but a little, I will come again.

ROMEO

O blessèd, blessèd night! I am afeard.
Being in night, all this is but a dream,
Too flattering-sweet to be substantial.

JULIET

Three words, dear Romeo, and good night indeed.
If that thy bent of love be honourable,
Thy purpose marriage, send me word to-morrow,
By one that I'll procure to come to thee,
Where and what time thou wilt perform the rite;
And all my fortunes at thy foot I'll lay
And follow thee my lord throughout the world.

NURSE [*Within*]

Madam!

JULIET

I come, anon.—But if thou mean'st not well,
I do beseech thee—

NURSE [*Within*]

Madam!

JULIET

By and by, I come:—
To cease thy suit, and leave me to my grief:
To-morrow will I send.

ROMEO

So thrive my soul—

JULIET

A thousand times good night!

ROMEO

A thousand times the worse, to want thy light.

Love goes toward love, as schoolboys from
    their books,
But love from love, toward school with heavy looks.
    [*Re-enter Juliet, above*]

JULIET

Hist! Romeo, hist! O, for a falconer's voice,
To lure this tassel-gentle back again!
Bondage is hoarse, and may not speak aloud;
Else would I tear the cave where Echo lies,
And make her airy tongue more hoarse than mine,
With repetition of my Romeo's name. Romeo!

ROMEO

It is my soul that calls upon my name:
How silver-sweet sound lovers' tongues by night,
Like softest music to attending ears!

JULIET

Romeo!

ROMEO

       My dear?

JULIET

              At what o'clock to-morrow
Shall I send to thee?

ROMEO

                   At the hour of nine.

JULIET

I will not fail: 'tis twenty years till then.
I have forgot why I did call thee back.

ROMEO

Let me stand here till thou remember it.

JULIET

I shall forget, to have thee still stand there,
Remembering how I love thy company.

ROMEO

And I'll still stay, to have thee still forget,
Forgetting any other home but this.

JULIET

'Tis almost morning; I would have thee gone:
And yet no further than a wanton's bird;

Who lets it hop a little from her hand,
Like a poor prisoner in his twisted gyves,
And with a silk thread plucks it back again,
So loving-jealous of his liberty.

ROMEO

I would I were thy bird.

JULIET

                    Sweet, so would I:
Yet I should kill thee with much cherishing.
Good night, good night! parting is such sweet
        sorrow,
That I shall say good night till it be morrow.

ROMEO

Sleep dwell upon thine eyes, peace in thy breast!
Would I were sleep and peace, so sweet to rest!
Hence will I to my ghostly father's cell,
His help to crave, and my dear hap to tell.

From *Romeo and Juliet*,
Act Two, scene 1

FRIAR LAURENCE

    Holy Saint Francis, what a change is here!
    Is Rosaline, whom thou didst love so dear,
    So soon forsaken? young men's love then lies
    Not truly in their hearts, but in their eyes.
    Jesu Maria, what a deal of brine
    Hath wash'd thy sallow cheeks for Rosaline!
    How much salt water thrown away in waste,
    To season love, that of it doth not taste!
    The sun not yet thy sighs from heaven clears,
    Thy old groans ring yet in my ancient ears;
    Lo, here upon thy cheek the stain doth sit
    Of an old tear that is not wash'd off yet:
    If e'er thou wast thyself and these woes thine,
    Thou and these woes were all for Rosaline:
    And art thou changed? pronounce this sentence
        then,
    Women may fall, when there's no strength in men.

ROMEO

    Thou chid'st me oft for loving Rosaline.

FRIAR LAURENCE

    For doting, not for loving, pupil mine.

ROMEO

    And bad'st me bury love.

FRIAR LAURENCE

                      Not in a grave,
    To lay one in, another out to have.

ROMEO

    I pray thee, chide not; she whom I love now
    Doth grace for grace and love for love allow;
    The other did not so.

FRIAR LAURENCE

                O, she knew well
    Thy love did read by rote and could not spell.
    But come, young waverer, come, go with me,
    In one respect I'll thy assistant be;
    For this alliance may so happy prove,
    To turn your households' rancour to pure love.

ROMEO

O, let us hence; I stand on sudden haste.

FRIAR LAURENCE

Wisely and slow; they stumble that run fast.

From *Romeo and Juliet*,
Act Two, scene 2

JULIET

Gallop apace, you fiery-footed steeds,
Towards Phoebus' lodging: such a wagoner
As Phaëthon would whip you to the west,
And bring in cloudy night immediately.
Spread thy close curtain, love-performing night,
That runaway's eyes may wink and Romeo
Leap to these arms, untalk'd of and unseen.
Lovers can see to do their amorous rites
By their own beauties; or, if love be blind,
It best agrees with night. Come, civil night,
Thou sober-suited matron, all in black,
And learn me how to lose a winning match,
Play'd for a pair of stainless maidenhoods:
Hood my unmann'd blood, bating in my cheeks,
With thy black mantle; till strange love, grown bold,
Think true love acted simple modesty.
Come, night; come, Romeo; come, thou day in
        night;
For thou wilt lie upon the wings of night
Whiter than new snow on a raven's back.
Come, gentle night, come, loving, black-brow'd
        night,
Give me my Romeo; and, when he shall die,
Take him and cut him out in little stars,
And he will make the face of heaven so fine
That all the world will be in love with night

And pay no worship to the garish sun.
O, I have bought the mansion of a love,
But not possess'd it, and, though I am sold,
Not yet enjoy'd: so tedious is this day
As is the night before some festival
To an impatient child that hath new robes
And may not wear them. O, here comes my nurse,
And she brings news; and every tongue that
    speaks
But Romeo's name speaks heavenly eloquence.

From *Romeo and Juliet*,
Act Three, scene 2

ROMEO
    'Tis torture, and not mercy: heaven is here,
Where Juliet lives; and every cat and dog
And little mouse, every unworthy thing,
Live here in heaven and may look on her;
But Romeo may not: more validity,
More honourable state, more courtship lives
In carrion-flies than Romeo: they my seize
On the white wonder of dear Juliet's hand
And steal immortal blessing from her lips,
Who even in pure and vestal modesty,
Still blush, as thinking their own kisses sin;
But Romeo may not; he is banishèd:
Flies may do this, but I from this must fly:
They are free men, but I am banishèd.
And say'st thou yet that exile is not death?
Hadst thou no poison mix'd, no sharp-ground knife,
No sudden mean of death, though ne'er so mean,
But 'banishèd' to kill me?—'banishèd'?
O friar, the damnèd use that word in hell;
Howlings attend it: how hast thou the heart,

Being a divine, a ghostly confessor,
A sin-absolver, and my friend profess'd,
To mangle me with that word 'banishèd'?

From *Romeo and Juliet*,
Act Three, scene 3

JULIET

Wilt thou be gone? it is not yet near day:
It was the nightingale, and not the lark,
That pierced the fearful hollow of thine ear;
Nightly she sings on yon pomegranate-tree:
Believe me, love, it was the nightingale.

ROMEO

It was the lark, the herald of the morn,
No nightingale: look, love, what envious streaks
Do lace the severing clouds in yonder east:
Night's candles are burnt out, and jocund day
Stands tiptoe on the misty mountain tops.
I must be gone and live, or stay and die.

JULIET

Yon light is not day-light, I know it, I:
It is some meteor that the sun exhales,
To be to thee this night a torch-bearer,
And light thee on thy way to Mantua:
Therefore stay yet; thou need'st not to be gone.

ROMEO

Let me be ta'en, let me be put to death;
I am content, so thou wilt have it so.
I'll say yon grey is not the morning's eye,
'Tis but the pale reflex of Cynthia's brow;
Nor that is not the lark, whose notes do beat
The vaulty heaven so high above our heads:
I have more care to stay than will to go:
Come, death, and welcome! Juliet wills it so.
How is't, my soul? let's talk; it is not day.

JULIET

It is, it is: hie hence, be gone, away!
It is the lark that sings so out of tune,
Straining harsh discords and unpleasing sharps.
Some say the lark makes sweet division;
This doth not so, for she divideth us:
Some say the lark and loathèd toad change eyes,
O, now I would they had changed voices too!
Since arm from arm that voice doth us affray,
Hunting thee hence with hunt's-up to the day,
O, now be gone; more light and light it grows.

ROMEO

More light and light; more dark and dark our woes!

NURSE

Madam!

JULIET

Nurse?

NURSE

Your lady mother is coming to your chamber:
The day is broke; be wary, look about.

JULIET

Then, window, let day in, and let life out.

ROMEO

Farewell, farewell! one kiss, and I'll descend.

JULIET

Art thou gone so? love, lord, ay, husband, friend!
I must hear from thee every day in the hour,
For in a minute there are many days:
O, by this count I shall be much in years
Ere I again behold my Romeo!

ROMEO

Farewell!
I will omit no opportunity
That may convey my greetings, love, to thee.

JULIET

O think'st thou we shall ever meet again?

ROMEO

I doubt it not; and all these woes shall serve
For sweet discourses in our time to come.

JULIET

O God, I have an ill-divining soul!
Methinks I see thee, now thou art below,
As one dead in the bottom of a tomb:
Either my eyesight fails, or thou look'st pale.

ROMEO

And trust me, love, in my eye so do you:
Dry sorrow drinks our blood. Adieu, adieu!

**From *Romeo and Juliet*,
Act Three, scene 5**

PAGE

O Lord, they fight! I will go call the watch.

PARIS

O, I am slain! If thou be merciful,
Open the tomb, lay me with Juliet.

ROMEO

In faith, I will. Let me peruse this face.
Mercutio's kinsman, noble County Paris!
What said my man, when my betossèd soul
Did not attend him as we rode? I think
He told me Paris should have married Juliet:
Said he not so? or did I dream it so?
Or am I mad, hearing him talk of Juliet,
To think it was so? O, give me thy hand,
One writ with me in sour misfortune's book!
I'll bury thee in a triumphant grave;
A grave? O no! a lantern, slaughter'd youth,
For here lies Juliet, and her beauty makes
This vault a feasting presence full of light.
Death, lie thou there, by a dead man interr'd.
How oft when men are at the point of death
Have they been merry! which their keepers call
A lightning before death: O, how may I

Call this a lightning? O my love! my wife!
Death, that hath suck'd the honey of thy breath,
Hath had no power yet upon thy beauty:
Thou art not conquer'd; beauty's ensign yet
Is crimson in thy lips and in thy cheeks,
And death's pale flag is not advanced there.
Tybalt, liest thou there in thy bloody sheet?
O, what more favour can I do to thee,
Than with that hand that cut thy youth in twain
To sunder his that was thine enemy?
Forgive me, cousin! Ah, dear Juliet,
Why art thou yet so fair? shall I believe
That unsubstantial death is amorous,
And that the lean abhorred monster keeps
Thee here in dark to be his paramour?
For fear of that, I still will stay with thee;
And never from this palace of dim night
Depart again: here, here will I remain
With worms that are thy chamber-maids; O, here
Will I set up my everlasting rest,
And shake the yoke of inauspicious stars
From this world-wearied flesh. Eyes, look your last!
Arms, take your last embrace! and, lips, O you
The doors of breath, seal with a righteous kiss
A dateless bargain to engrossing death!
Come, bitter conduct, come, unsavoury guide!
Thou desperate pilot, now at once run on
The dashing rocks thy sea-sick weary bark!
Here's to my love! O true apothecary!
Thy drugs are quick. Thus with a kiss I die.

From *Romeo and Juliet*,
Act Five, scene 3

ANTONIO

But little: I am arm'd and well prepared.
Give me your hand, Bassanio: fare you well!
Grieve not that I am fallen to this for you;
For herein Fortune shows herself more kind
Than is her custom: it is still her use
To let the wretched man outlive his wealth,
To view with hollow eye and wrinkled brow
An age of poverty; from which lingering penance
Of such misery doth she cut me off.
Commend me to your honourable wife:
Tell her the process of Antonio's end;
Say how I loved you, speak me fair in death;
And, when the tale is told, bid her be judge
Whether Bassanio had not once a love.
Repent but you that you shall lose your friend,
And he repents not that he pays your debt;
For if the Jew do cut but deep enough,
I'll pay it presently with all my heart.

BASSANIO

Antonio, I am married to a wife
Which is as dear to me as life itself;
But life itself, my wife, and all the world,
Are not with me esteem'd above thy life:
I would lose all, ay, sacrifice them all
Here to this devil, to deliver you.

PORTIA

Your wife would give you little thanks for that,
If she were by, to hear you make the offer.

**From *The Merchant of Venice*,
Act 4, scene 1**

BOY

Signior?

BENEDICK

In my chamber-window lies a book: bring it hither to me in the orchard.

BOY

I am here already, sir.

BENEDICK

I know that; but I would have thee hence, and here again.

[*Exit Boy*]

I do much wonder that one man, seeing how much another man is a fool when he dedicates his behaviors to love, will, after he hath laughed at such shallow follies in others, become the argument of his own scorn by falling in love: and such a man is Claudio. I have known when there was no music with him but the drum and the fife; and now had he rather hear the tabour and the pipe: I have known when he would have walked ten mile a-foot to see a good armour; and now will he lie ten nights awake, carving the fashion of a new doublet. He was wont to speak plain and to the purpose, like an honest man and a soldier; and now is he turned orthography; his words are a very fantastical banquet, just so many strange dishes. May I be so converted and see with these eyes? I cannot tell; I think not: I will not be sworn, but love may transform me to an oyster; but I'll take my oath on it, till he have made an oyster of me, he shall never make me such a fool. One woman is fair, yet I am well; another is wise, yet I am well; another virtuous, yet I am well; but till all graces be in one woman, one woman shall not come in my

grace. Rich she shall be, that's certain; wise,
or I'll none; virtuous, or I'll never cheapen her;
fair, or I'll never look on her; mild, or come not
near me; noble, or not I for an angel; of good
discourse, an excellent musician, and her hair
shall be of what colour it please God.

. . . .

BALTHASAR

    Sigh no more, ladies, sigh no more,
      Men were deceivers ever,
    One foot in sea and one on shore,
      To one thing constant never:
    Then sigh not so, but let them go,
      And be you blithe and bonny,
    Converting all your sounds of woe
      Into hey nonny, nonny.

    Sing no more ditties, sing no moe,
      Of dumps so dull and heavy;
    The fraud of men was ever so,
      Since summer first was leafy:
    Then sigh not so, but let them go,
      And be you blithe and bonny,
    Converting all your sounds of woe
      Into hey nonny, nonny.

. . . .

BENEDICK

    [*Coming forward*]

    This can be no trick: the conference was sadly
borne. They have the truth of this from Hero.
They seem to pity the lady: it seems her affec-
tions have their full bent. Love me! why, it must
be requited. I hear how I am censured: they say
I will bear myself proudly, if I perceive the love
come from her; they say too that she will
rather die than give any sign of affection.

I did never think to marry: I must not seem proud: happy are they that hear their detractions and can put them to mending. They say the lady is fair; 'tis a truth, I can bear them witness; and virtuous; 'tis so, I cannot reprove it; and wise, but for loving me; by my troth, it is no addition to her wit, nor no great argument of her folly, for I will be horribly in love with her. I may chance have some odd quirks and remnants of wit broken on me, because I have railed so long against marriage: but doth not the appetite alter? a man loves the meat in his youth that he cannot endure in his age. Shall quips and sentences and these paper bullets of the brain awe a man from the career of his humour? No, the world must be peopled. When I said I would die a bachelor, I did not think I should live till I were married. Here comes Beatrice. By this day! she's a fair lady: I do spy some marks of love in her.

[*Enter Beatrice*]

**From *Much Ado About Nothing*,
Act Two, scene 3**

BENEDICK
Lady Beatrice, have you wept all this while?
BEATRICE
Yea, and I will weep a while longer.
BENEDICK
I will not desire that.
BEATRICE
You have no reason; I do it freely.
BENEDICK
Surely I do believe your fair cousin is wronged.

BEATRICE

Ah, how much might the man deserve of me
that would right her!

BENEDICK

Is there any way to show such friendship?

BEATRICE

A very even way, but no such friend.

BENEDICK

May a man do it?

BEATRICE

It is a man's office, but not yours.

BENEDICK

I do love nothing in the world so well as you:
is not that strange?

BEATRICE

As strange as the thing I know not. It were as
possible for me to say I loved nothing so well
as you: but believe me not; and yet I lie not; I
confess nothing, nor I deny nothing. I am sorry
for my cousin.

BENEDICK

By my sword, Beatrice, thou lovest me.

BEATRICE

Do not swear, and eat it.

BENEDICK

I will swear by it that you love me; and I will
make him eat it that says I love not you.

BEATRICE

Will you not eat your word?

BENEDICK

With no sauce that can be devised to it. I
protest I love thee.

BEATRICE

Why, then, God forgive me!

BENEDICK

What offence, sweet Beatrice?

BEATRICE

You have stayed me in a happy hour: I was
about to protest I loved you.

BENEDICK

And do it with all thy heart.

BEATRICE

I love you with so much of my heart that none
is left to protest.

BENEDICK

Come, bid me do any thing for thee.

BEATRICE

Kill Claudio.

BENEDICK

Ha! not for the wide world.

BEATRICE

You kill me to deny it. Farewell.

BENEDICK

Tarry, sweet Beatrice.

BEATRICE

I am gone, though I am here: there is no love
in you: nay, I pray you, let me go.

BENEDICK

Beatrice,—

BEATRICE

In faith, I will go.

BENEDICK

We'll be friends first.

BEATRICE

You dare easier be friends with me than fight
with mine enemy.

BENEDICK

Is Claudio thine enemy?

BEATRICE

Is he not approved in the height a villain, that
hath slandered, scorned, dishonoured my
kinswoman? O that I were a man! What, bear
her in hand until they come to take hands; and
then, with public accusation, uncovered slan-
der, unmitigated rancour,—O God, that I were
a man! I would eat his heart in the market-
place.

BENEDICK

Hear me, Beatrice,—

BEATRICE

Talk with a man out at a window! A proper saying!

BENEDICK

Nay, but, Beatrice,—

BEATRICE

Sweet Hero! She is wronged, she is slandered, she is undone.

BENEDICK

Beat—

BEATRICE

Princes and counties! Surely, a princely testimony, a goodly count, Count Comfect; a sweet gallant, surely! O that I were a man for his sake! or that I had any friend would be a man for my sake! But manhood is melted into courtesies, valour into compliment, and men are only turned into tongue, and trim ones too: he is now as valiant as Hercules that only tells a lie and swears it. I cannot be a man with wishing, therefore I will die a woman with grieving.

BENEDICK

Tarry, good Beatrice. By this hand, I love thee.

BEATRICE

Use it for my love some other way than swearing by it.

BENEDICK

Think you in your soul the Count Claudio hath wronged Hero?

BEATRICE

Yea, as sure as I have a thought or a soul.

BENEDICK

Enough, I am engaged; I will challenge him. I will kiss your hand, and so I leave you. By this hand, Claudio shall render me a dear account. As you hear of me, so think of me. Go, comfort your cousin: I must say she is dead: and so, farewell.

From *Much Ado About Nothing*,
Act Four, scene 1

SILVIUS

O Corin, that thou knew'st how I do love her!

CORIN

I partly guess; for I have loved ere now.

SILVIUS

No, Corin, being old, thou canst not guess,
Though in thy youth thou wast as true a lover
As ever sigh'd upon a midnight pillow:
But if thy love were ever like to mine—
As sure I think did never man love so—
How many actions most ridiculous
Hast thou been drawn to by thy fantasy?

CORIN

Into a thousand that I have forgotten.

SILVIUS

O, thou didst then ne'er love so heartily!
If thou remember'st not the slightest folly
That ever love did make thee run into,
Thou hast not loved:
Or if thou hast not sat as I do now,
Wearying thy hearer in thy mistress' praise,
Thou hast not loved:
Or if thou hast not broke from company
Abruptly, as my passion now makes me,
Thou hast not loved.
O Phebe, Phebe, Phebe!

[*Exit*]

ROSALIND

Alas, poor shepherd! searching of thy wound,
I have by hard adventure found mine own.

TOUCHSTONE

And I mine. I remember, when I was in love I
broke my sword upon a stone and bid him take
that for coming a-night to Jane Smile; and I
remember the kissing of her batlet and the
cow's dugs that her pretty chopt hands had
milked; and I remember the wooing of a peas-
cod instead of her, from whom I took two cods

and, giving her them again, said with weeping tears, 'Wear these for my sake.' We that are true lovers run into strange capers; but as all is mortal in nature, so is all nature in love mortal in folly.

From *As You Like It*,
Act Two, scene 3

[*Enter Orlando, with a paper*]

ORLANDO

Hang there, my verse, in witness of my love:
    And thou, thrice-crownèd queen of night, survey
With thy chaste eye, from thy pale sphere above,
    Thy huntress' name that my full life doth sway.
O Rosalind! these trees shall be my books
    And in their barks my thoughts I'll character;
That every eye which in this forest looks
    Shall see thy virtue witness'd every where.
Run, run, Orlando; carve on every tree
The fair, the chaste and unexpressive she.

.   .   .   .

[*Enter Rosalind, with a paper, reading*]

ROSALIND

From the east to western Ind,
No jewel is like Rosalind.
Her worth, being mounted on the wind,
Through all the world bears Rosalind.
All the pictures fairest lined
Are but black to Rosalind.
Let no fair be kept in mind
But the fair of Rosalind.

TOUCHSTONE

I'll rhyme you so eight years together, dinners and suppers and sleeping-hours excepted: it is the right butter-women's rank to market.

ROSALIND

Out, fool!

TOUCHSTONE

For a taste:

If a hart do lack a hind,
Let him seek out Rosalind.
If the cat will after kind,
So be sure will Rosalind.
Winter garments must be lined,
So must slender Rosalind.
They that reap must sheaf and bind;
Then to cart with Rosalind.
Sweetest nut hath sourest rind,
Such a nut is Rosalind.
He that sweetest rose will find
Must find love's prick and Rosalind.

This is the very false gallop of verses: why do you infect yourself with them?

ROSALIND

Peace, you dull fool! I found them on a tree.

TOUCHSTONE

Truly, the tree yields bad fruit.

ROSALIND

I'll graff it with you, and then I shall graff it with a medlar: then it will be the earliest fruit i' the country; for you'll be rotten ere you be half ripe, and that's the right virtue of the medlar.

.   .   .   .

JAQUES

I thank you for your company; but, good faith, I had as lief have been myself alone.

ORLANDO

And so had I; but yet, for fashion sake, I thank you too for your society.

JAQUES

God be wi' you: let's meet as little as we can.

ORLANDO

I do desire we may be better strangers.

JAQUES

I pray you, mar no more trees with writing love-songs in their barks.

ORLANDO

I pray you, mar no more of my verses with reading them ill-favouredly.

JAQUES

Rosalind is your love's name?

ORLANDO

Yes, just.

JAQUES

I do not like her name.

ORLANDO

There was no thought of pleasing you when she was christened.

JAQUES

What stature is she of?

ORLANDO

Just as high as my heart.

JAQUES

You are full of pretty answers. Have you not been acquainted with goldsmiths' wives, and conned them out of rings?

ORLANDO

Not so; but I answer you right painted cloth, from whence you have studied your questions.

JAQUES

You have a nimble wit: I think 'twas made of Atalanta's heels. Will you sit down with me? and we two will rail against our mistress the world and all our misery.

ORLANDO

I will chide no breather in the world but myself, against whom I know most faults.

JAQUES

The worst fault you have is to be in love.

ORLANDO

'Tis a fault I will not change for your best virtue. I am weary of you.

JAQUES

By my troth, I was seeking for a fool when I found you.

ORLANDO

He is drowned in the brook: look but in, and you shall see him.

JAQUES

There I shall see mine own figure.

ORLANDO

Which I take to be either a fool or a cipher.

JAQUES

I'll tarry no longer with you: farewell, good Signior Love.

. . . .

ORLANDO

Can you remember any of the principal evils that he laid to the charge of women?

ROSALIND

There were none principal; they were all like one another as half-pence are, every one fault seeming monstrous till his fellow fault came to match it.

ORLANDO

I prithee, recount some of them.

ROSALIND

No, I will not cast away my physic but on those that are sick. There is a man haunts the forest, that abuses our young plants with carving 'Rosalind' on their barks; hangs odes upon hawthorns and elegies on brambles, all, forsooth, deifying the name of Rosalind: if I could meet that fancy-monger I would give him some good counsel, for he seems to have the quotidian of love upon him.

ORLANDO

I am he that is so love-shaked: I pray you tell me your remedy.

ROSALIND

There is none of my uncle's marks upon you:
he taught me how to know a man in love; in
which cage of rushes I am sure you are not
prisoner.

ORLANDO

What were his marks?

ROSALIND

A lean cheek, which you have not, a blue eye
and sunken, which you have not, an unques-
tionable spirit, which you have not, a beard
neglected, which you have not; but I pardon
you for that, for simply your having in beard is
a younger brother's revenue: then your hose
should be ungartered, your bonnet unbanded,
your sleeve unbuttoned, your shoe untied and
every thing about you demonstrating a careless
desolation; but you are no such man; you are
rather point-device in your accoutrements as
loving yourself than seeming the lover of any
other.

ORLANDO

Fair youth, I would I could make thee believe
I love.

ROSALIND

Me believe it! you may as soon make her that
you love believe it; which, I warrant, she is
apter to do than to confess she does: that is one
of the points in which the women still give the
lie to their consciences. But, in good sooth, are
you he that hangs the verses on the trees,
wherein Rosalind is so admired?

ORLANDO

I swear to thee, youth, by the white hand of
Rosalind, I am that he, that unfortunate he.

ROSALIND

But are you so much in love as your rhymes
speak?

ORLANDO

Neither rhyme nor reason can express how much.

ROSALIND

Love is merely a madness, and, I tell you, deserves as well a dark house and a whip as madmen do: and the reason why they are not so punished and cured is, that the lunacy is so ordinary that the whippers are in love too. Yet I profess curing it by counsel.

ORLANDO

Did you ever cure any so?

ROSALIND

Yes, one, and in this manner. He was to imagine me his love, his mistress; and I set him every day to woo me: at which time would I, being but a moonish youth, grieve, be effeminate, changeable, longing and liking, proud, fantastical, apish, shallow, inconstant, full of tears, full of smiles, for every passion something and for no passion truly any thing, as boys and women are for the most part cattle of this colour; would now like him, now loathe him; then entertain him, then forswear him; now weep for him, then spit at him; that I drave my suitor from his mad humour of love to a living humour of madness; which was, to forswear the full stream of the world, and to live in a nook merely monastic. And thus I cured him; and this way will I take upon me to wash your liver as clean as a sound sheep's heart, that there shall not be one spot of love in't.

ORLANDO

I would not be cured, youth.

ROSALIND

I would cure you, if you would but call me Rosalind and come every day to my cot, and woo me.

ORLANDO

Now, by the faith of my love, I will: tell me where it is.

ROSALIND

Go with me to it and I'll show it you and by the way you shall tell me where in the forest you live. Will you go?

ORLANDO

With all my heart, good youth.

ROSALIND

Nay you must call me Rosalind. Come, sister, will you go?

**From *As You Like It*,
Act Three, scene 2**

ROSALIND

Never talk to me; I will weep.

CELIA

Do, I prithee; but yet have the grace to consider that tears do not become a man.

ROSALIND

But have I not cause to weep?

CELIA

As good cause as one would desire; therefore weep.

ROSALIND

His very hair is of the dissembling colour.

CELIA

Something browner than Judas's. Marry, his kisses are Judas's own children.

ROSALIND

I' faith, his hair is of a good colour.

CELIA

An excellent colour: your chestnut was ever the only colour.

ROSALIND

And his kissing is as full of sanctity as the
touch of holy bread.

CELIA

He hath bought a pair of cast lips of Diana: a
nun of winter's sisterhood kisses not more reli-
giously; the very ice of chastity is in them.

ROSALIND

But why did he swear he would come this
morning, and comes not?

CELIA

Nay, certainly, there is no truth in him.

ROSALIND

Do you think so?

CELIA

Yes; I think he is not a pick-purse nor a horse-
stealer, but for his verity in love, I do think
him as concave as a covered goblet or a worm-
eaten nut.

ROSALIND

Not true in love?

CELIA

Yes, when he is in; but I think he is not in.

ROSALIND

You have heard him swear downright he was.

CELIA

'Was' is not 'is.' Besides, the oath of a lover is
no stronger than the word of a tapster; they are
both the confirmer of false reckonings. He
attends here in the forest on the duke your
father.

ROSALIND

I met the duke yesterday and had much ques-
tion with him: he asked me of what parentage
I was; I told him, of as good as he; so he
laughed and let me go. But what talk we of
fathers, when there is such a man as Orlando?

CELIA

O, that's a brave man! he writes brave verses, speaks brave words, swears brave oaths and breaks them bravely, quite traverse, athwart the heart of his lover; as a puny tilter, that spurs his horse but on one side, breaks his staff like a noble goose: but all's brave that youth mounts and folly guides.

**From *As You Like It*,
Act Three, scene 4**

ROSALIND

You must begin, 'Will you, Orlando—'

CELIA

Go to. Will you, Orlando, have to wife this Rosalind?

ORLANDO

I will.

ROSALIND

Ay, but when?

ORLANDO

Why now; as fast as she can marry us.

ROSALIND

Then you must say 'I take thee, Rosalind, for wife.'

ORLANDO

I take thee, Rosalind, for wife.

ROSALIND

I might ask you for your commission; but I do take thee, Orlando, for my husband: there's a girl goes before the priest; and certainly a woman's thought runs before her actions.

ORLANDO

So do all thoughts; they are winged.

ROSALIND

Now tell me how long you would have her after you have possessed her.

ORLANDO

For ever and a day.

ROSALIND

Say 'a day,' without the 'ever.' No, no, Orlando; men are April when they woo, December when they wed: maids are May when they are maids, but the sky changes when they are wives. I will be more jealous of thee than a Barbary cock-pigeon over his hen, more clamorous than a parrot against rain, more new-fangled than an ape, more giddy in my desires than a monkey: I will weep for nothing, like Diana in the fountain, and I will do that when you are disposed to be merry; I will laugh like a hyena, and that when thou art inclined to sleep.

ORLANDO

But will my Rosalind do so?

ROSALIND

By my life, she will do as I do.

ORLANDO

O, but she is wise.

ROSALIND

Or else she could not have the wit to do this: the wiser, the waywarder: make the doors upon a woman's wit and it will out at the casement; shut that and 'twill out at the key-hole; stop that, 'twill fly with the smoke out at the chimney.

ORLANDO

A man that had a wife with such a wit, he might say 'Wit, whither wilt?'

ROSALIND

Nay, you might keep that cheque for it till you met your wife's wit going to your neighbour's bed.

ORLANDO

And what wit could wit have to excuse that?

ROSALIND

Marry, to say she came to seek you there. You
shall never take her without her answer, unless
you take her without her tongue. O, that
woman that cannot make her fault her hus-
band's occasion, let her never nurse her child
herself, for she will breed it like a fool!

ORLANDO

For these two hours, Rosalind, I will leave
thee.

ROSALIND

Alas! dear love, I cannot lack thee two hours.

ORLANDO

I must attend the duke at dinner: by two
o'clock I will be with thee again.

ROSALIND

Ay, go your ways, go your ways; I knew what
you would prove: my friends told me as much,
and I thought no less: that flattering tongue of
yours won me: 'tis but one cast away, and so,
come, death! Two o'clock is your hour?

ORLANDO

Ay, sweet Rosalind.

ROSALIND

By my troth, and in good earnest, and so God
mend me, and by all pretty oaths that are not
dangerous, if you break one jot of your promise
or come one minute behind your hour, I will
think you the most pathetical break-promise
and the most hollow lover and the most unwor-
thy of her you call Rosalind that may be cho-
sen out of the gross band of the unfaithful:
therefore beware my censure and keep your
promise.

ORLANDO

With no less religion than if thou wert indeed
my Rosalind: so adieu.

ROSALIND

Well, Time is the old justice that examines all
such offenders, and let Time try: adieu.
[*Exit Orlando*]

**From *As You Like It*,
Act Four, scene 1**

Duke Orsino

If music be the food of love, play on;
Give me excess of it, that, surfeiting,
The appetite may sicken, and so die.
That strain again! it had a dying fall:
O, it came o'er my ear like the sweet sound,
That breathes upon a bank of violets,
Stealing and giving odour! Enough; no more:
'Tis not so sweet now as it was before.
O spirit of love! how quick and fresh art thou,
That, notwithstanding thy capacity
Receiveth as the sea, nought enters there,
Of what validity and pitch so e'er,
But falls into abatement and low price,
Even in a minute: so full of shapes is fancy
That it alone is high fantastical.

**From *Twelfth Night*,
Act One, scene 1**

Viola

I left no ring with her: what means this lady?
Fortune forbid my outside have not charm'd her!
She made good view of me; indeed, so much,
That sure methought her eyes had lost her
        tongue,
For she did speak in starts distractedly.
She loves me, sure; the cunning of her passion
Invites me in this churlish messenger.
None of my lord's ring! why, he sent her none.
I am the man: if it be so, as 'tis,
Poor lady, she were better love a dream.
Disguise, I see, thou art a wickedness,
Wherein the pregnant enemy does much.

How easy is it for the proper-false
In women's waxen hearts to set their forms!
Alas, our frailty is the cause, not we!
For such as we are made of, such we be.
How will this fadge? my master loves her dearly;
And I, poor monster, fond as much on him;
And she, mistaken, seems to dote on me.
What will become of this? As I am man,
My state is desperate for my master's love;
As I am woman,—now alas the day!—
What thriftless sighs shall poor Olivia breathe!
O time! thou must untangle this, not I;
It is too hard a knot for me to untie!

From *Twelfth Night*,
Act Two, scene 2

FESTE
   [*Sings*]
   O mistress mine, where are you roaming?
   O, stay and hear; your true love's coming,
      That can sing both high and low:
   Trip no further, pretty sweeting;
   Journeys end in lovers meeting,
      Every wise man's son doth know.

   . . . .

   What is love? 'tis not hereafter;
   Present mirth hath present laughter;
      What's to come is still unsure:
   In delay there lies no plenty;
   Then come kiss me, sweet and twenty,
      Youth's a stuff will not endure.

From *Twelfth Night*,
Act Two, scene 3

FESTE

[*Sings*]

Come away, come away, death,
   And in sad cypress let me be laid;
Fly away, fly away breath;
   I am slain by a fair cruel maid.
My shroud of white, stuck all with yew,
      O, prepare it!
My part of death, no one so true
      Did share it.

Not a flower, not a flower sweet
   On my black coffin let there be strewn;
Not a friend, not a friend greet
   My poor corpse, where my bones shall be
      thrown:
A thousand thousand sighs to save,
      Lay me, O, where
Sad true lover never find my grave,
      To weep there!

      .   .   .   .

DUKE ORSINO

There is no woman's sides
Can bide the beating of so strong a passion
As love doth give my heart; no woman's heart
So big, to hold so much; they lack retention
Alas, their love may be call'd appetite,
No motion of the liver, but the palate,
That suffer surfeit, cloyment and revolt;
But mine is all as hungry as the sea,
And can digest as much: make no compare
Between that love a woman can bear me
And that I owe Olivia.

VIOLA

Ay, but I know—

DUKE ORSINO

What dost thou know?

VIOLA

Too well what love women to men may owe:

In faith, they are as true of heart as we.
My father had a daughter loved a man,
As it might be, perhaps, were I a woman,
I should your lordship.

DUKE ORSINO

            And what's her history?

VIOLA

A blank, my lord. She never told her love,
But let concealment, like a worm i' the bud,
Feed on her damask cheek: she pined in
    thought,
And with a green and yellow melancholy
She sat like patience on a monument,
Smiling at grief. Was not this love indeed?
We men may say more, swear more: but indeed
Our shows are more than will; for still we
    prove
Much in our vows, but little in our love.

DUKE ORSINO

But died thy sister of her love, my boy?

VIOLA

I am all the daughters of my father's house,
And all the brothers too: and yet I know not.
Sir, shall I to this lady?

DUKE ORSINO

            Ay, that's the theme.
To her in haste; give her this jewel; say,
My love can give no place, bide no denay.

**From *Twelfth Night*,
Act Two, scene 4**

DUKE ORSINO
   Why should I not, had I the heart to do it,
   Like to the Egyptian thief at point of death,
   Kill what I love?—a savage jealousy
   That sometimes savours nobly. But hear me this:
   Since you to non-regardance cast my faith,
   And that I partly know the instrument
   That screws me from my true place in your favour,
   Live you the marble-breasted tyrant still;
   But this your minion, whom I know you love,
   And whom, by heaven I swear, I tender dearly,
   Him will I tear out of that cruel eye,
   Where he sits crownèd in his master's spite.
   Come, boy, with me; my thoughts are ripe in
       mischief:
   I'll sacrifice the lamb that I do love,
   To spite a raven's heart within a dove.

From *Twelfth Night*,
Act Five, scene 1

TROILUS

    I take to-day a wife, and my election
Is led on in the conduct of my will;
My will enkindled by mine eyes and ears,
Two traded pilots 'twixt the dangerous shores
Of will and judgment: how may I avoid,
Although my will distaste what it elected,
The wife I chose? there can be no evasion
To blench from this and to stand firm by honour:
We turn not back the silks upon the merchant,
When we have soil'd them, nor the remainder
      viands
We do not throw in unrespective sewer,
Because we now are full. It was thought meet
Paris should do some vengeance on the Greeks:
Your breath of full consent bellied his sails;
The seas and winds, old wranglers, took a truce
And did him service: he touch'd the ports desired,
And for an old aunt whom the Greeks held
      captive,
He brought a Grecian queen, whose youth and
      freshness
Wrinkles Apollo's, and makes stale the morning.
Why keep we her? the Grecians keep our aunt:
Is she worth keeping? why, she is a pearl,
Whose price hath launch'd above a thousand
      ships,
And turn'd crown'd kings to merchants.
If you'll avouch 'twas wisdom Paris went—
As you must needs, for you all cried 'Go, go,'—
If you'll confess he brought home noble prize—
As you must needs, for you all clapp'd your hands
And cried 'Inestimable!'—why do you now
The issue of your proper wisdoms rate,
And do a deed that fortune never did,
Beggar the estimation which you prized
Richer than sea and land? O, theft most base,
That we have stol'n what we do fear to keep!

But, thieves, unworthy of a thing so stol'n,
That in their country did them that disgrace,
We fear to warrant in our native place!

**From *Troilus and Cressida*,
Act Two, scene 2**

PANDARUS
In good troth, it begins so.
[*Sings*]
Love, love, nothing but love, still love, still more!
For, O, love's bow
Shoots buck and doe:
The shaft confounds,
Not that it wounds,
But tickles still the sore.
These lovers cry Oh! oh! they die!
Yet that which seems the wound to kill,
Doth turn oh! oh! to ha! ha! he!
So dying love lives still:
Oh! oh! a while, but ha! ha! ha!
Oh! oh! groans out for ha! ha! ha!
Heigh-ho!
HELEN
In love, i' faith, to the very tip of the nose.
PARIS
He eats nothing but doves, love, and that
breeds hot blood, and hot blood begets hot
thoughts, and hot thoughts beget hot deeds,
and hot deeds is love.
PANDARUS
Is this the generation of love? hot blood, hot
thoughts, and hot deeds? Why, they are vipers:
is love a generation of vipers?

**From *Troilus and Cressida*,
Act Three, scene 1**

TROILUS

I am giddy; expectation whirls me round.
The imaginary relish is so sweet
That it enchants my sense: what will it be,
When that the watery palate tastes indeed
Love's thrice repurèd nectar? Death, I fear me,
Swooning destruction, or some joy too fine,
Too subtle-potent, tuned too sharp in sweetness,
For the capacity of my ruder powers:
I fear it much; and I do fear besides,
That I shall lose distinction in my joys;
As doth a battle, when they charge on heaps
The enemy flying.

. . . .

CRESSIDA

They say all lovers swear more performance
than they are able and yet reserve an ability that
they never perform, vowing more than the per-
fection of ten and discharging less than the tenth
part of one. They that have the voice of lions and
the act of hares, are they not monsters?

TROILUS

Are there such? such are not we: praise us as
we are tasted, allow us as we prove; our head
shall go bare till merit crown it: no perfection
in reversion shall have a praise in present: we
will not name desert before his birth, and,
being born, his addition shall be humble. Few
words to fair faith: Troilus shall be such to
Cressid as what envy can say worst shall be a
mock for his truth, and what truth can speak
truest not truer than Troilus.

From *Troilus and Cressida*,
Act Three, scene 2

Sonnets

1

From fairest creatures we desire increase,
That thereby beauty's rose might never die,
But as the riper should by time decease,
His tender heir might bear his memory:
But thou, contracted to thine own bright eyes,
Feed'st thy light'st flame with self-substantial fuel,
Making a famine where abundance lies,
Thyself thy foe, to thy sweet self too cruel.
Thou that art now the world's fresh ornament
And only herald to the gaudy spring,
Within thine own bud buriest thy content
And, tender churl, makest waste in niggarding.
    Pity the world, or else this glutton be,
      To eat the world's due, by the grave and thee.

2

When forty winters shall beseige thy brow,
And dig deep trenches in thy beauty's field,
Thy youth's proud livery, so gazed on now,
Will be a tatter'd weed, of small worth held:
Then being ask'd where all thy beauty lies,
Where all the treasure of thy lusty days,
To say, within thine own deep-sunken eyes,
Were an all-eating shame and thriftless praise.
How much more praise deserved thy beauty's use,
If thou couldst answer 'This fair child of mine
Shall sum my count and make my old excuse,'
Proving his beauty by succession thine!
    This were to be new made when thou art old,
      And see thy blood warm when thou feel'st it cold.

3

Look in thy glass, and tell the face thou viewest
Now is the time that face should form another;
Whose fresh repair if now thou not renewest,
Thou dost beguile the world, unbless some mother.
For where is she so fair whose unear'd womb
Disdains the tillage of thy husbandry?
Or who is he so fond will be the tomb
Of his self-love, to stop posterity?
Thou art thy mother's glass, and she in thee
Calls back the lovely April of her prime:
So thou through windows of thine age shall see
Despite of wrinkles this thy golden time.
 But if thou live, remember'd not to be,
  Die single, and thine image dies with thee.

4

Unthrifty loveliness, why dost thou spend
Upon thyself thy beauty's legacy?
Nature's bequest gives nothing but doth lend,
And being frank she lends to those are free.
Then, beauteous niggard, why dost thou abuse
The bounteous largess given thee to give?
Profitless usurer, why dost thou use
So great a sum of sums, yet canst not live?
For having traffic with thyself alone,
Thou of thyself thy sweet self dost deceive.
Then how, when nature calls thee to be gone,
What acceptable audit canst thou leave?
 Thy unused beauty must be tomb'd with thee,
  Which, usèd, lives th' executor to be.

5

Those hours, that with gentle work did frame
The lovely gaze where every eye doth dwell,
Will play the tyrants to the very same
And that unfair which fairly doth excel:
For never-resting time leads summer on
To hideous winter and confounds him there;
Sap cheque'd with frost and lusty leaves quite gone,
Beauty o'ersnow'd and bareness every where:
Then, were not summer's distillation left,
A liquid prisoner pent in walls of glass,
Beauty's effect with beauty were bereft,
Nor it nor no remembrance what it was:
    But flowers distill'd though they with winter meet,
    Lose but their show; their substance still lives
        sweet.

6

Then let not winter's ragged hand deface
In thee thy summer, ere thou be distill'd:
Make sweet some vial; treasure thou some place
With beauty's treasure, ere it be self-kill'd.
That use is not forbidden usury,
Which happies those that pay the willing loan;
That's for thyself to breed another thee,
Or ten times happier, be it ten for one;
Ten times thyself were happier than thou art,
If ten of thine ten times refigured thee:
Then what could death do, if thou shouldst depart,
Leaving thee living in posterity?
    Be not self-will'd, for thou art much too fair
    To be death's conquest and make worms thine
        heir.

7

Lo! in the orient when the gracious light
Lifts up his burning head, each under eye
Doth homage to his new-appearing sight,
Serving with looks his sacred majesty;
And having climb'd the steep-up heavenly hill,
Resembling strong youth in his middle age,
Yet mortal looks adore his beauty still,
Attending on his golden pilgrimage;
But when from highmost pitch, with weary car,
Like feeble age, he reeleth from the day,
The eyes, 'fore duteous, now converted are
From his low tract and look another way:
    So thou, thyself out-going in thy noon,
      Unlook'd on diest, unless thou get a son.

8

Music to hear, why hear'st thou music sadly?
Sweets with sweets war not, joy delights in joy.
Why lovest thou that which thou receivest not gladly,
Or else receivest with pleasure thine annoy?
If the true concord of well-tunèd sounds,
By unions married, do offend thine ear,
They do but sweetly chide thee, who confounds
In singleness the parts that thou shouldst bear.
Mark how one string, sweet husband to another,
Strikes each in each by mutual ordering,
Resembling sire and child and happy mother
Who all in one, one pleasing note do sing:
    Whose speechless song, being many, seeming
        one,
      Sings this to thee: 'thou single wilt prove none.'

9

Is it for fear to wet a widow's eye
That thou consumest thyself in single life?
Ah! if thou issueless shalt hap to die.
The world will wail thee, like a makeless wife;
The world will be thy widow and still weep
That thou no form of thee hast left behind,
When every private widow well may keep
By children's eyes her husband's shape in mind.
Look, what an unthrift in the world doth spend
Shifts but his place, for still the world enjoys it;
But beauty's waste hath in the world an end,
And kept unused, the user so destroys it.
   No love toward others in that bosom sits
   That on himself such murderous shame
      commits.

10

For shame! deny that thou bear'st love to any,
Who for thyself art so unprovident.
Grant, if thou wilt, thou art beloved of many,
But that thou none lovest is most evident;
For thou art so possess'd with murderous hate
That 'gainst thyself thou stick'st not to conspire.
Seeking that beauteous roof to ruinate
Which to repair should be thy chief desire.
O, change thy thought, that I may change my mind!
Shall hate be fairer lodged than gentle love?
Be, as thy presence is, gracious and kind,
Or to thyself at least kind-hearted prove:
   Make thee another self, for love of me,
   That beauty still may live in thine or thee.

11

As fast as thou shalt wane, so fast thou growest
In one of thine, from that which thou departest;
And that fresh blood which youngly thou bestowest
Thou mayst call thine when thou from youth
  convertest.
Herein lives wisdom, beauty and increase:
Without this, folly, age and cold decay:
If all were minded so, the times should cease
And threescore year would make the world away.
Let those whom Nature hath not made for store,
Harsh featureless and rude, barrenly perish:
Look, whom she best endow'd she gave the more;
Which bounteous gift thou shouldst in bounty
  cherish:
  She carved thee for her seal, and meant thereby
  Thou shouldst print more, not let that copy die.

12

When I do count the clock that tells the time,
And see the brave day sunk in hideous night;
When I behold the violet past prime,
And sable curls all silver'd o'er with white;
When lofty trees I see barren of leaves
Which erst from heat did canopy the herd,
And summer's green all girded up in sheaves
Borne on the bier with white and bristly beard,
Then of thy beauty do I question make,
That thou among the wastes of time must go,
Since sweets and beauties do themselves forsake
And die as fast as they see others grow;
  And nothing 'gainst Time's scythe can make
    defence
  Save breed, to brave him when he takes thee
    hence.

13

O, that you were yourself! but, love, you are
No longer yours than you yourself here live:
Against this coming end you should prepare,
And your sweet semblance to some other give.
So should that beauty which you hold in lease
Find no determination: then you were
Yourself again after yourself's decease,
When your sweet issue your sweet form should bear.
Who lets so fair a house fall to decay,
Which husbandry in honour might uphold
Against the stormy gusts of winter's day
And barren rage of death's eternal cold?
    O, none but unthrifts! Dear my love, you know
    You had a father: let your son say so.

14

Not from the stars do I my judgment pluck;
And yet methinks I have astronomy,
But not to tell of good or evil luck,
Of plagues, of dearths, or seasons' quality;
Nor can I fortune to brief minutes tell,
Pointing to each his thunder, rain and wind,
Or say with princes if it shall go well,
By oft predict that I in heaven find:
But from thine eyes my knowledge I derive,
And, constant stars, in them I read such art
As truth and beauty shall together thrive,
If from thyself to store thou wouldst convert;
    Or else of thee this I prognosticate:
    Thy end is truth's and beauty's doom and date.

15

When I consider every thing that grows
Holds in perfection but a little moment,
That this huge stage presenteth nought but shows
Whereon the stars in secret influence comment;
When I perceive that men as plants increase,
Cheerèd and cheque'd even by the self-same sky,
Vaunt in their youthful sap, at height decrease,
And wear their brave state out of memory;
Then the conceit of this inconstant stay
Sets you most rich in youth before my sight,
Where wasteful Time debateth with Decay,
To change your day of youth to sullied night;
    And all in war with Time for love of you,
    As he takes from you, I engraft you new.

16

But wherefore do not you a mightier way
Make war upon this bloody tyrant, Time?
And fortify yourself in your decay
With means more blessèd than my barren rhyme?
Now stand you on the top of happy hours,
And many maiden gardens yet unset
With virtuous wish would bear your living flowers,
Much liker than your painted counterfeit:
So should the lines of life that life repair,
Which this, Time's pencil, or my pupil pen,
Neither in inward worth nor outward fair,
Can make you live yourself in eyes of men.
    To give away yourself keeps yourself still,
    And you must live, drawn by your own sweet
        skill.

17

Who will believe my verse in time to come,
If it were fill'd with your most high deserts?
Though yet, heaven knows, it is but as a tomb
Which hides your life and shows not half your parts.
If I could write the beauty of your eyes
And in fresh numbers number all your graces,
The age to come would say 'This poet lies:
Such heavenly touches ne'er touch'd earthly faces.'
So should my papers yellow'd with their age
Be scorn'd like old men of less truth than tongue,
And your true rights be term'd a poet's rage
And stretchèd metre of an antique song:
    But were some child of yours alive that time,
    You should live twice; in it and in my rhyme.

18

Shall I compare thee to a summer's day?
Thou art more lovely and more temperate:
Rough winds do shake the darling buds of May,
And summer's lease hath all too short a date:
Sometime too hot the eye of heaven shines,
And often is his gold complexion dimm'd;
And every fair from fair sometime declines,
By chance or nature's changing course untrimm'd;
But thy eternal summer shall not fade
Nor lose possession of that fair thou owest;
Nor shall Death brag thou wander'st in his shade,
When in eternal lines to time thou growest:
    So long as men can breathe or eyes can see,
    So long lives this and this gives life to thee.

19

Devouring Time, blunt thou the lion's paws,
And make the earth devour her own sweet brood;
Pluck the keen teeth from the fierce tiger's jaws,
And burn the long-lived phoenix in her blood;
Make glad and sorry seasons as thou fleets,
And do whate'er thou wilt, swift-footed Time,
To the wide world and all her fading sweets;
But I forbid thee one most heinous crime:
O, carve not with thy hours my love's fair brow,
Nor draw no lines there with thine antique pen;
Him in thy course untainted do allow
For beauty's pattern to succeeding men.
    Yet, do thy worst, old Time: despite thy wrong,
    My love shall in my verse ever live young.

20

A woman's face with Nature's own hand painted
Hast thou, the master-mistress of my passion;
A woman's gentle heart, but not acquainted
With shifting change, as is false women's fashion;
An eye more bright than theirs, less false in rolling,
Gilding the object whereupon it gazeth;
A man in hue, all 'hues' in his controlling,
Much steals men's eyes and women's souls amazeth.
And for a woman wert thou first created;
Till Nature, as she wrought thee, fell a-doting,
And by addition me of thee defeated,
By adding one thing to my purpose nothing.
    But since she prick'd thee out for women's
        pleasure,
    Mine be thy love and thy love's use their
        treasure.

21

So is it not with me as with that Muse
Stirr'd by a painted beauty to his verse,
Who heaven itself for ornament doth use
And every fair with his fair doth rehearse
Making a couplement of proud compare,
With sun and moon, with earth and sea's rich gems,
With April's first-born flowers, and all things rare
That heaven's air in this huge rondure hems.
O let me, true in love, but truly write,
And then believe me, my love is as fair
As any mother's child, though not so bright
As those gold candles fix'd in heaven's air:
    Let them say more than like of hearsay well;
    I will not praise that purpose not to sell.

22

My glass shall not persuade me I am old,
So long as youth and thou are of one date;
But when in thee time's furrows I behold,
Then look I death my days should expiate.
For all that beauty that doth cover thee
Is but the seemly raiment of my heart,
Which in thy breast doth live, as thine in me:
How can I then be elder than thou art?
O, therefore, love, be of thyself so wary
As I, not for myself, but for thee will;
Bearing thy heart, which I will keep so chary
As tender nurse her babe from faring ill.
    Presume not on thy heart when mine is slain;
    Thou gavest me thine, not to give back again.

23

As an unperfect actor on the stage
Who with his fear is put besides his part,
Or some fierce thing replete with too much rage,
Whose strength's abundance weakens his own heart.
So I, for fear of trust, forget to say
The perfect ceremony of love's rite,
And in mine own love's strength seem to decay,
O'ercharged with burden of mine own love's might.
O, let my books be then the eloquence
And dumb presagers of my speaking breast,
Who plead for love and look for recompense
More than that tongue that more hath more
        express'd.
    O, learn to read what silent love hath writ:
    To hear with eyes belongs to love's fine wit.

24

Mine eye hath play'd the painter and hath stell'd
Thy beauty's form in table of my heart;
My body is the frame wherein 'tis held,
And perspective it is the painter's art.
For through the painter must you see his skill,
To find where your true image pictured lies;
Which in my bosom's shop is hanging still,
That hath his windows glazèd with thine eyes.
Now see what good turns eyes for eyes have done:
Mine eyes have drawn thy shape, and thine for me
Are windows to my breast, where-through the sun
Delights to peep, to gaze therein on thee;
    Yet eyes this cunning want to grace their art;
    They draw but what they see, know not the heart.

25

Let those who are in favour with their stars
Of public honour and proud titles boast,
Whilst I, whom fortune of such triumph bars,
Unlook'd for joy in that I honour most.
Great princes' favourites their fair leaves spread
But as the marigold at the sun's eye,
And in themselves their pride lies burièd,
For at a frown they in their glory die.
The painful warrior famousèd for might,
After a thousand victories once foil'd,
Is from the book of honour razèd quite,
And all the rest forgot for which he toil'd:
　　Then happy I, that love and am beloved
　　Where I may not remove nor be removed.

26

Lord of my love, to whom in vassalage
Thy merit hath my duty strongly knit,
To thee I send this written embassage,
To witness duty, not to show my wit:
Duty so great, which wit so poor as mine
May make seem bare, in wanting words to show it,
But that I hope some good conceit of thine
In thy soul's thought, all naked, will bestow it;
Till whatsoever star that guides my moving
Points on me graciously with fair aspect
And puts apparel on my tatter'd loving,
To show me worthy of thy sweet respect:
　　Then may I dare to boast how I do love thee;
　　Till then not show my head where thou mayst
　　　　prove me.

29

When, in disgrace with fortune and men's eyes,
I all alone beweep my outcast state
And trouble deaf heaven with my bootless cries
And look upon myself and curse my fate,
Wishing me like to one more rich in hope,
Featured like him, like him with friends possess'd,
Desiring this man's art and that man's scope,
With what I most enjoy contented least;
Yet in these thoughts myself almost despising,
Haply I think on thee, and then my state,
Like to the lark at break of day arising
From sullen earth, sings hymns at heaven's gate;
    For thy sweet love remember'd such wealth
        brings
    That then I scorn to change my state with kings.

30

When to the sessions of sweet silent thought
I summon up remembrance of things past,
I sigh the lack of many a thing I sought,
And with old woes new wail my dear time's waste:
Then can I drown an eye, unused to flow,
For precious friends hid in death's dateless night,
And weep afresh love's long since cancell'd woe,
And moan the expense of many a vanish'd sight:
Then can I grieve at grievances foregone,
And heavily from woe to woe tell o'er
The sad account of fore-bemoanèd moan,
Which I new pay as if not paid before.
    But if the while I think on thee, dear friend,
    All losses are restored and sorrows end.

31

Thy bosom is endearèd with all hearts,
Which I by lacking have supposèd dead,
And there reigns love and all love's loving parts,
And all those friends which I thought burièd.
How many a holy and obsequious tear
Hath dear religious love stol'n from mine eye
As interest of the dead, which now appear
But things removed that hidden in thee lie!
Thou art the grave where buried love doth live,
Hung with the trophies of my lovers gone,
Who all their parts of me to thee did give;
That due of many now is thine alone:
    Their images I loved I view in thee,
    And thou, all they, hast all the all of me.

32

If thou survive my well-contented day,
When that churl Death my bones with dust shall
      cover,
And shalt by fortune once more re-survey
These poor rude lines of thy deceasèd lover,
Compare them with the bettering of the time,
And though they be outstripp'd by every pen,
Reserve them for my love, not for their rhyme,
Exceeded by the height of happier men.
O, then vouchsafe me but this loving thought:
'Had my friend's Muse grown with this growing age,
A dearer birth than this his love had brought,
To march in ranks of better equipage:
    But since he died and poets better prove,
    Theirs for their style I'll read, his for his love.'

35

No more be grieved at that which thou hast done:
Roses have thorns, and silver fountains mud;
Clouds and eclipses stain both moon and sun,
And loathsome canker lives in sweetest bud.
All men make faults, and even I in this,
Authorizing thy trespass with compare,
Myself corrupting, salving thy amiss,
Excusing thy sins more than thy sins are;
For to thy sensual fault I bring in sense—
Thy adverse party is thy advocate—
And 'gainst myself a lawful plea commence:
Such civil war is in my love and hate
    That I an accessary needs must be
    To that sweet thief which sourly robs from me.

36

Let me confess that we two must be twain,
Although our undivided loves are one:
So shall those blots that do with me remain
Without thy help by me be borne alone.
In our two loves there is but one respect,
Though in our lives a separable spite,
Which though it alter not love's sole effect,
Yet doth it steal sweet hours from love's delight.
I may not evermore acknowledge thee,
Lest my bewailèd guilt should do thee shame,
Nor thou with public kindness honour me,
Unless thou take that honour from thy name:
    But do not so; I love thee in such sort
    As, thou being mine, mine is thy good report.

37

As a decrepit father takes delight
To see his active child do deeds of youth,
So I, made lame by fortune's dearest spite,
Take all my comfort of thy worth and truth.
For whether beauty, birth, or wealth, or wit,
Or any of these all, or all, or more,
Entitled in thy parts do crownèd sit,
I make my love engrafted to this store:
So then I am not lame, poor, nor despised,
Whilst that this shadow doth such substance give
That I in thy abundance am sufficed
And by a part of all thy glory live.
　　Look, what is best, that best I wish in thee:
　　This wish I have; then ten times happy me!

38

How can my Muse want subject to invent,
While thou dost breathe, that pour'st into my verse
Thine own sweet argument, too excellent
For every vulgar paper to rehearse?
O, give thyself the thanks, if aught in me
Worthy perusal stand against thy sight;
For who's so dumb that cannot write to thee,
When thou thyself dost give invention light?
Be thou the tenth Muse, ten times more in worth
Than those old nine which rhymers invocate;
And he that calls on thee, let him bring forth
Eternal numbers to outlive long date.
　　If my slight Muse do please these curious days,
　　The pain be mine, but thine shall be the praise.

39

O, how thy worth with manners may I sing,
When thou art all the better part of me?
What can mine own praise to mine own self bring?
And what is 't but mine own when I praise thee?
Even for this let us divided live,
And our dear love lose name of single one,
That by this separation I may give
That due to thee which thou deservest alone.
O absence, what a torment wouldst thou prove,
Were it not thy sour leisure gave sweet leave
To entertain the time with thoughts of love,
Which time and thoughts so sweetly doth deceive,
   And that thou teachest how to make one twain,
   By praising him here who doth hence remain!

40

Take all my loves, my love, yea, take them all;
What hast thou then more than thou hadst before?
No love, my love, that thou mayst true love call;
All mine was thine before thou hadst this more.
Then if for my love thou my love receivest,
I cannot blame thee for my love thou usest;
But yet be blamed, if thou thyself deceivest
By wilful taste of what thyself refusest.
I do forgive thy robbery, gentle thief,
Although thou steal thee all my poverty;
And yet, love knows, it is a greater grief
To bear love's wrong than hate's known injury.
   Lascivious grace, in whom all ill well shows,
   Kill me with spites; yet we must not be foes.

41

Those petty wrongs that liberty commits,
When I am sometime absent from thy heart,
Thy beauty and thy years full well befits,
For still temptation follows where thou art.
Gentle thou art and therefore to be won,
Beauteous thou art, therefore to be assailed;
And when a woman woos, what woman's son
Will sourly leave her till she have prevailed?
Ay me! but yet thou mightest my seat forbear,
And chide try beauty and thy straying youth,
Who lead thee in their riot even there
Where thou art forced to break a twofold truth,
    Hers by thy beauty tempting her to thee,
    Thine, by thy beauty being false to me.

42

That thou hast her, it is not all my grief,
And yet it may be said I loved her dearly;
That she hath thee, is of my wailing chief,
A loss in love that touches me more nearly.
Loving offenders, thus I will excuse ye:
Thou dost love her, because thou knowst I love her;
And for my sake even so doth she abuse me,
Suffering my friend for my sake to approve her.
If I lose thee, my loss is my love's gain,
And losing her, my friend hath found that loss;
Both find each other, and I lose both twain,
And both for my sake lay on me this cross:
    But here's the joy; my friend and I are one;
    Sweet flattery! then she loves but me alone.

43

When most I wink, then do mine eyes best see,
For all the day they view things unrespected;
But when I sleep, in dreams they look on thee,
And darkly bright are bright in dark directed.
Then thou, whose shadow shadows doth make
      bright,
How would thy shadow's form form happy show
To the clear day with thy much clearer light,
When to unseeing eyes thy shade shines so!
How would, I say, mine eyes be blessèd made
By looking on thee in the living day,
When in dead night thy fair imperfect shade
Through heavy sleep on sightless eyes doth stay!
    All days are nights to see till I see thee,
    And nights bright days when dreams do show
        thee me.

44

If the dull substance of my flesh were thought,
Injurious distance should not stop my way;
For then despite of space I would be brought,
From limits far remote where thou dost stay.
No matter then although my foot did stand
Upon the farthest earth removed from thee;
For nimble thought can jump both sea and land
As soon as think the place where he would be.
But ah! thought kills me that I am not thought,
To leap large lengths of miles when thou art gone,
But that so much of earth and water wrought
I must attend time's leisure with my moan,
    Receiving nought by elements so slow
    But heavy tears, badges of either's woe.

45

The other two, slight air and purging fire,
Are both with thee, wherever I abide;
The first my thought, the other my desire,
These present-absent with swift motion slide.
For when these quicker elements are gone
In tender embassy of love to thee,
My life, being made of four, with two alone
Sinks down to death, oppress'd with melancholy;
Until life's composition be recured
By those swift messengers return'd from thee,
Who even but now come back again, assured
Of thy fair health, recounting it to me:
    This told, I joy; but then no longer glad,
    I send them back again and straight grow sad.

46

Mine eye and heart are at a mortal war
How to divide the conquest of thy sight;
Mine eye my heart thy picture's sight would bar,
My heart mine eye the freedom of that right.
My heart doth plead that thou in him dost lie—
A closet never pierced with crystal eyes—
But the defendant doth that plea deny
And says in him thy fair appearance lies.
To 'cide this title is impannelèd
A quest of thoughts, all tenants to the heart,
And by their verdict is determinèd
The clear eye's moiety and the dear heart's part:
    As thus; mine eye's due is thy outward part,
    And my heart's right thy inward love of heart.

54

O, how much more doth beauty beauteous seem
By that sweet ornament which truth doth give!
The rose looks fair, but fairer we it deem
For that sweet odour which doth in it live.
The canker-blooms have full as deep a dye
As the perfumèd tincture of the roses,
Hang on such thorns and play as wantonly
When summer's breath their maskèd buds discloses:
But, for their virtue only is their show,
They live unwoo'd and unrespected fade,
Die to themselves. Sweet roses do not so;
Of their sweet deaths are sweetest odours made:
    And so of you, beauteous and lovely youth,
    When that shall fade, my verse distills your
        truth.

55

Not marble, nor the gilded monuments
Of princes, shall outlive this powerful rhyme;
But you shall shine more bright in these contents
Than unswept stone besmear'd with sluttish time.
When wasteful war shall statues overturn,
And broils root out the work of masonry,
Nor Mars his sword nor war's quick fire shall burn
The living record of your memory.
'Gainst death and all-oblivious enmity
Shall you pace forth; your praise shall still find room
Even in the eyes of all posterity
That wear this world out to the ending doom.
    So, till the judgment that yourself arise,
    You live in this, and dwell in lover's eyes.

57

Being your slave, what should I do but tend
Upon the hours and times of your desire?
I have no precious time at all to spend,
Nor services to do, till you require.
Nor dare I chide the world-without-end hour
Whilst I, my sovereign, watch the clock for you,
Nor think the bitterness of absence sour
When you have bid your servant once adieu;
Nor dare I question with my jealous thought
Where you may be, or your affairs suppose,
But, like a sad slave, stay and think of nought
Save, where you are how happy you make those.
    So true a fool is love that in your will,
    Though you do any thing, he thinks no ill.

58

That god forbid that made me first your slave,
I should in thought control your times of pleasure,
Or at your hand the account of hours to crave,
Being your vassal, bound to stay your leisure!
O, let me suffer, being at your beck,
The imprison'd absence of your liberty;
And patience, tame to sufferance, bide each cheque,
Without accusing you of injury.
Be where you list, your charter is so strong
That you yourself may privilege your time
To what you will; to you it doth belong
Yourself to pardon of self-doing crime.
    I am to wait, though waiting so be hell;
    Not blame your pleasure, be it ill or well.

60

Like as the waves make towards the pebbled shore,
So do our minutes hasten to their end;
Each changing place with that which goes before,
In sequent toil all forwards do contend.
Nativity, once in the main of light,
Crawls to maturity, wherewith being crown'd,
Crookèd elipses 'gainst his glory fight,
And Time that gave doth now his gift confound.
Time doth transfix the flourish set on youth
And delves the parallels in beauty's brow,
Feeds on the rarities of nature's truth,
And nothing stands but for his scythe to mow:
    And yet to times in hope my verse shall stand,
    Praising thy worth, despite his cruel hand.

61

Is it thy will thy image should keep open
My heavy eyelids to the weary night?
Dost thou desire my slumbers should be broken,
While shadows like to thee do mock my sight?
Is it thy spirit that thou send'st from thee
So far from home into my deeds to pry,
To find out shames and idle hours in me,
The scope and tenor of thy jealousy?
O, no! thy love, though much, is not so great:
It is my love that keeps mine eye awake;
Mine own true love that doth my rest defeat,
To play the watchman ever for thy sake:
    For thee watch I whilst thou dost wake elsewhere,
    From me far off, with others all too near.

62

Sin of self-love possesseth all mine eye
And all my soul and all my every part;
And for this sin there is no remedy,
It is so grounded inward in my heart.
Methinks no face so gracious is as mine,
No shape so true, no truth of such account;
And for myself mine own worth do define,
As I all other in all worths surmount.
But when my glass shows me myself indeed,
Beated and chopp'd with tann'd antiquity,
Mine own self-love quite contrary I read;
Self so self-loving were iniquity.
    'Tis thee, myself, that for myself I praise,
    Painting my age with beauty of thy days.

63

Against my love shall be, as I am now,
With Time's injurious hand crush'd and o'er-worn;
When hours have drain'd his blood and fill'd his
      brow
With lines and wrinkles; when his youthful morn
Hath travell'd on to age's steepy night,
And all those beauties whereof now he's king
Are vanishing or vanish'd out of sight,
Stealing away the treasure of his spring;
For such a time do I now fortify
Against confounding age's cruel knife,
That he shall never cut from memory
My sweet love's beauty, though my lover's life:
    His beauty shall in these black lines be seen,
    And they shall live, and he in them still green.

64

When I have seen by Time's fell hand defaced
The rich proud cost of outworn buried age;
When sometime lofty towers I see down-razed
And brass eternal slave to mortal rage;
When I have seen the hungry ocean gain
Advantage on the kingdom of the shore,
And the firm soil win of the watery main,
Increasing store with loss and loss with store;
When I have seen such interchange of state,
Or state itself confounded to decay;
Ruin hath taught me thus to ruminate,
That Time will come and take my love away.
   This thought is as a death, which cannot choose
   But weep to have that which it fears to lose.

65

Since brass, nor stone, nor earth, nor boundless
     sea,
But sad mortality o'er-sways their power,
How with this rage shall beauty hold a plea,
Whose action is no stronger than a flower?
O, how shall summer's honey breath hold out
Against the wrackful siege of battering days,
When rocks impregnable are not so stout,
Nor gates of steel so strong, but Time decays?
O fearful meditation! where, alack,
Shall Time's best jewel from Time's chest lie hid?
Or what strong hand can hold his swift foot back?
Or who his spoil of beauty can forbid?
   O, none, unless this miracle have might,
   That in black ink my love may still shine bright.

66

Tired with all these, for restful death I cry,
As, to behold desert a beggar born,
And needy nothing trimm'd in jollity,
And purest faith unhappily forsworn,
And guilded honour shamefully misplaced,
And maiden virtue rudely strumpeted,
And right perfection wrongfully disgraced,
And strength by limping sway disablèd,
And art made tongue-tied by authority,
And folly doctor-like controlling skill,
And simple truth miscall'd simplicity,
And captive good attending captain ill:
    Tired with all these, from these would I be gone,
    Save that, to die, I leave my love alone.

69

Those parts of thee that the world's eye doth view
Want nothing that the thought of hearts can mend;
All tongues, the voice of souls, give thee that due,
Uttering bare truth, even so as foes commend.
Thy outward thus with outward praise is crown'd;
But those same tongues that give thee so thine own
In other accents do this praise confound
By seeing farther than the eye hath shown.
They look into the beauty of thy mind,
And that, in guess, they measure by thy deeds;
Then, churls, their thoughts, although their eyes
    were kind,
To thy fair flower add the rank smell of weeds:
    But why thy odour matcheth not thy show,
    The solve is this, that thou dost common grow.

71

No longer mourn for me when I am dead
Then you shall hear the surly sullen bell
Give warning to the world that I am fled
From this vile world, with vilest worms to dwell:
Nay, if you read this line, remember not
The hand that writ it; for I love you so
That I in your sweet thoughts would be forgot
If thinking on me then should make you woe.
O, if, I say, you look upon this verse
When I perhaps compounded am with clay,
Do not so much as my poor name rehearse.
But let your love even with my life decay,
　　Lest the wise world should look into your moan
　　And mock you with me after I am gone.

72

O, lest the world should task you to recite
What merit lived in me, that you should love
After my death, dear love, forget me quite,
For you in me can nothing worthy prove;
Unless you would devise some virtuous lie,
To do more for me than mine own desert,
And hang more praise upon deceasèd I
Than niggard truth would willingly impart:
O, lest your true love may seem false in this,
That you for love speak well of me untrue,
My name be buried where my body is,
And live no more to shame nor me nor you.
　　For I am shamed by that which I bring forth,
　　And so should you, to love things nothing worth.

73

That time of year thou mayst in me behold
When yellow leaves, or none, or few, do hang
Upon those boughs which shake against the cold,
Bare ruin'd choirs, where late the sweet birds sang.
In me thou seest the twilight of such day
As after sunset fadeth in the west,
Which by and by black night doth take away,
Death's second self, that seals up all in rest.
In me thou see'st the glowing of such fire
That on the ashes of his youth doth lie,
As the death-bed whereon it must expire
Consumed with that which it was nourish'd by.
    This thou perceivest, which makes thy love
        more strong,
    To love that well which thou must leave ere
        long.

74

But be contented: when that fell arrest
Without all bail shall carry me away,
My life hath in this line some interest,
Which for memorial still with thee shall stay.
When thou reviewest this, thou dost review
The very part was consecrate to thee:
The earth can have but earth, which is his due;
My spirit is thine, the better part of me:
So then thou hast but lost the dregs of life,
The prey of worms, my body being dead,
The coward conquest of a wretch's knife,
Too base of thee to be rememberèd.
    The worth of that is that which it contains,
    And that is this, and this with thee remains.

75

So are you to my thoughts as food to life,
Or as sweet-season'd showers are to the ground;
And for the peace of you I hold such strife
As 'twixt a miser and his wealth is found;
Now proud as an enjoyer and anon
Doubting the filching age will steal his treasure,
Now counting best to be with you alone,
Then better'd that the world may see my pleasure;
Sometime all full with feasting on your sight
And by and by clean starvèd for a look;
Possessing or pursuing no delight,
Save what is had or must from you be took.
   Thus do I pine and surfeit day by day,
    Or gluttoning on all, or all away.

76

Why is my verse so barren of new pride,
So far from variation or quick change?
Why with the time do I not glance aside
To new-found methods and to compounds strange?
Why write I still all one, ever the same,
And keep invention in a noted weed,
That every word doth almost tell my name,
Showing their birth and where they did proceed?
O, know, sweet love, I always write of you,
And you and love are still my argument;
So all my best is dressing old words new,
Spending again what is already spent:
   For as the sun is daily new and old,
    So is my love still telling what is told.

79

Whilst I alone did call upon thy aid,
My verse alone had all thy gentle grace,
But now my gracious numbers are decay'd
And my sick Muse doth give another place.
I grant, sweet love, thy lovely argument
Deserves the travail of a worthier pen,
Yet what of thee thy poet doth invent
He robs thee of and pays it thee again.
He lends thee virtue and he stole that word
From thy behavior; beauty doth he give
And found it in thy cheek; he can afford
No praise to thee but what in thee doth live.
　　Then thank him not for that which he doth say,
　　Since what he owes thee thou thyself dost pay.

80

O, how I faint when I of you do write,
Knowing a better spirit doth use your name,
And in the praise thereof spends all his might,
To make me tongue-tied, speaking of your fame!
But since your worth, wide as the ocean is,
The humble as the proudest sail doth bear,
My saucy bark inferior far to his
On your broad main doth wilfully appear.
Your shallowest help will hold me up afloat,
Whilst he upon your soundless deep doth ride;
Or being wreck'd, I am a worthless boat,
He of tall building and of goodly pride:
　　Then if he thrive and I be cast away,
　　The worst was this; my love was my decay.

81

Or I shall live your epitaph to make,
Or you survive when I in earth am rotten;
From hence your memory death cannot take,
Although in me each part will be forgotten.
Your name from hence immortal life shall have,
Though I, once gone, to all the world must die:
The earth can yield me but a common grave,
When you entombèd in men's eyes shall lie.
Your monument shall be my gentle verse,
Which eyes not yet created shall o'er-read,
And tongues to be your being shall rehearse
When all the breathers of this world are dead;
   You still shall live—such virtue hath my pen—
   Where breath most breathes, even in the
      mouths of men.

87

Farewell! thou art too dear for my possessing,
And like enough thou know'st thy estimate:
The charter of thy worth gives thee releasing;
My bonds in thee are all determinate.
For how do I hold thee but by thy granting?
And for that riches where is my deserving?
The cause of this fair gift in me is wanting,
And so my patent back again is swerving.
Thyself thou gavest, thy own worth then not knowing,
Or me, to whom thou gavest it, else mistaking;
So thy great gift, upon misprision growing,
Comes home again, on better judgment making.
   Thus have I had thee, as a dream doth flatter,
   In sleep a king, but waking no such matter.

89

Say that thou didst forsake me for some fault,
And I will comment upon that offence;
Speak of my lameness, and I straight will halt,
Against thy reasons making no defence.
Thou canst not, love, disgrace me half so ill,
To set a form upon desirèd change,
As I'll myself disgrace: knowing thy will,
I will acquaintance strangle and look strange,
Be absent from thy walks, and in my tongue
Thy sweet belovèd name no more shall dwell,
Lest I, too much profane, should do it wrong
And haply of our old acquaintance tell.
    For thee against myself I'll vow debate,
    For I must ne'er love him whom thou dost hate.

91

Some glory in their birth, some in their skill,
Some in their wealth, some in their bodies' force,
Some in their garments, though new-fangled ill,
Some in their hawks and hounds, some in their
    horse;
And every humour hath his adjunct pleasure,
Wherein it finds a joy above the rest:
But these particulars are not my measure;
All these I better in one general best.
Thy love is better than high birth to me,
Richer than wealth, prouder than garments' cost,
Of more delight than hawks or horses be;
And having thee, of all men's pride I boast:
    Wretched in this alone, that thou mayst take
    All this away and me most wretched make.

93

So shall I live, supposing thou art true,
Like a deceivèd husband; so love's face
May still seem love to me, though alter'd new;
Thy looks with me, thy heart in other place:
For there can live no hatred in thine eye,
Therefore in that I cannot know thy change.
In many's looks the false heart's history
Is writ in moods and frowns and wrinkles strange,
But heaven in thy creation did decree
That in thy face sweet love should ever dwell;
Whate'er thy thoughts or thy heart's workings be,
Thy looks should nothing thence but sweetness tell.
    How like Eve's apple doth thy beauty grow,
      if thy sweet virtue answer not thy show!

94

They that have power to hurt and will do none,
That do not do the thing they most do show,
Who, moving others, are themselves as stone,
Unmovèd, cold, and to temptation slow,
They rightly do inherit heaven's graces
And husband nature's riches from expense;
They are the lords and owners of their faces,
Others but stewards of their excellence.
The summer's flower is to the summer sweet,
Though to itself it only live and die,
But if that flower with base infection meet,
The basest weed outbraves his dignity:
    For sweetest things turn sourest by their deeds;
      Lilies that fester smell far worse than weeds.

95

How sweet and lovely dost thou make the shame
Which, like a canker in the fragrant rose,
Doth spot the beauty of thy budding name!
O, in what sweets dost thou thy sins enclose!
That tongue that tells the story of thy days,
Making lascivious comments on thy sport,
Cannot dispraise but in a kind of praise;
Naming thy name blesses an ill report.
O, what a mansion have those vices got
Which for their habitation chose out thee,
Where beauty's veil doth cover every blot,
And all things turn to fair that eyes can see!
   Take heed, dear heart, of this large privilege;
   The hardest knife ill-used doth lose his edge.

105

Let not my love be call'd idolatry,
Nor my belovèd as an idol show,
Since all alike my songs and praises be
To one, of one, still such, and ever so.
Kind is my love to-day, to-morrow kind,
Still constant in a wondrous excellence;
Therefore my verse to constancy confined,
One thing expressing, leaves out difference.
'Fair, kind and true' is all my argument,
'Fair, kind, and true' varying to other words;
And in this change is my invention spent,
Three themes in one, which wondrous scope
   affords.
   'Fair, kind, and true,' have often lived alone,
   Which three till now never kept seat in one.

106

When in the chronicle of wasted time
I see descriptions of the fairest wights,
And beauty making beautiful old rhyme
In praise of ladies dead and lovely knights,
Then, in the blazon of sweet beauty's best,
Of hand, of foot, of lip, of eye, of brow,
I see their antique pen would have express'd
Even such a beauty as you master now.
So all their praises are but prophecies
Of this our time, all you prefiguring;
And, for they look'd but with divining eyes,
They had not skill enough your worth to sing:
　　For we, which now behold these present days,
　　Had eyes to wonder, but lack tongues to praise.

107

Not mine own fears, nor the prophetic soul
Of the wide world dreaming on things to come,
Can yet the lease of my true love control,
Supposed as forfeit to a confined doom.
The mortal moon hath her eclipse endured
And the sad augurs mock their own presage;
Incertainties now crown themselves assured
And peace proclaims olives of endless age.
Now with the drops of this most balmy time
My love looks fresh, and death to me subscribes,
Since, spite of him, I'll live in this poor rhyme,
While he insults o'er dull and speechless tribes:
　　And thou in this shalt find thy monument,
　　When tyrants' crests and tombs of brass are
　　　　spent.

108

What's in the brain that ink may character
Which hath not figured to thee my true spirit?
What's new to speak, what new to register,
That may express my love or thy dear merit?
Nothing, sweet boy; but yet, like prayers divine,
I must, each day say o'er the very same,
Counting no old thing old, thou mine, I thine,
Even as when first I hallow'd thy fair name.
So that eternal love in love's fresh case
Weighs not the dust and injury of age,
Nor gives to necessary wrinkles place,
But makes antiquity for aye his page,
    Finding the first conceit of love there bred
    Where time and outward form would show it
       dead.

109

O, never say that I was false of heart,
Though absence seem'd my flame to qualify.
As easy might I from myself depart
As from my soul, which in thy breast doth lie:
That is my home of love: if I have ranged,
Like him that travels I return again,
Just to the time, not with the time exchanged,
So that myself bring water for my stain.
Never believe, though in my nature reign'd
All frailties that besiege all kinds of blood,
That it could so preposterously be stain'd,
To leave for nothing all thy sum of good;
    For nothing this wide universe I call,
    Save thou, my rose; in it thou art my all.

111

O, for my sake do you with Fortune chide,
The guilty goddess of my harmful deeds,
That did not better for my life provide
Than public means which public manners breeds.
Thence comes it that my name receives a brand,
And almost thence my nature is subdued
To what it works in, like the dyer's hand:
Pity me then and wish I were renew'd;
Whilst, like a willing patient, I will drink
Potions of eisel 'gainst my strong infection
No bitterness that I will bitter think,
Nor double penance, to correct correction.
    Pity me then, dear friend, and I assure ye
    Even that your pity is enough to cure me.

116

Let me not to the marriage of true minds
Admit impediments. Love is not love
Which alters when it alteration finds,
Or bends with the remover to remove:
O no! it is an ever-fixèd mark
That looks on tempests and is never shaken;
It is the star to every wandering bark,
Whose worth's unknown, although his height be
        taken.
Love's not Time's fool, though rosy lips and cheeks
Within his bending sickle's compass come:
Love alters not with his brief hours and weeks,
But bears it out even to the edge of doom.
    If this be error and upon me proved,
    I never writ, nor no man ever loved.

129

The expense of spirit in a waste of shame
Is lust in action; and till action, lust
Is perjured, murderous, bloody, full of blame,
Savage, extreme, rude, cruel, not to trust,
Enjoy'd no sooner but despisèd straight,
Past reason hunted, and no sooner had
Past reason hated, as a swallow'd bait
On purpose laid to make the taker mad;
Mad in pursuit and in possession so;
Had, having, and in quest to have, extreme;
A bliss in proof, and proved, a very woe;
Before, a joy proposed; behind, a dream.
    All this the world well knows; yet none knows
        well
    To shun the heaven that leads men to this hell.

130

My mistress' eyes are nothing like the sun;
Coral is far more red than her lips' red;
If snow be white, why then her breasts are dun;
If hairs be wires, black wires grow on her head.
I have seen roses damask'd, red and white,
But no such roses see I in her cheeks;
And in some perfumes is there more delight
Than in the breath that from my mistress reeks.
I love to hear her speak, yet well I know
That music hath a far more pleasing sound;
I grant I never saw a goddess go;
My mistress, when she walks, treads on the ground:
    And yet, by heaven, I think my love as rare
    As any she belied with false compare.

131

Thou art as tyrannous, so as thou art,
As those whose beauties proudly make them cruel;
For well thou know'st to my dear doting heart
Thou art the fairest and most precious jewel.
Yet, in good faith, some say that thee behold
Thy face hath not the power to make love groan:
To say they err I dare not be so bold,
Although I swear it to myself alone.
And, to be sure that is not false I swear,
A thousand groans, but thinking on thy face,
One on another's neck, do witness bear
Thy black is fairest in my judgment's place.
    In nothing art thou black save in thy deeds,
    And thence this slander, as I think, proceeds.

132

Thine eyes I love, and they, as pitying me,
Knowing thy heart torments me with disdain,
Have put on black and loving mourners be,
Looking with pretty ruth upon my pain.
And truly not the morning sun of heaven
Better becomes the grey cheeks of the east,
Nor that full star that ushers in the even
Doth half that glory to the sober west,
As those two mourning eyes become thy face:
O, let it then as well beseem thy heart
To mourn for me, since mourning doth thee
    grace,
And suit thy pity like in every part.
    Then will I swear beauty herself is black
    And all they foul that thy complexion lack.

133

Beshrew that heart that makes my heart to groan
For that deep wound it gives my friend and me!
Is't not enough to torture me alone,
But slave to slavery my sweet'st friend must be?
Me from myself thy cruel eye hath taken,
And my next self thou harder hast engross'd:
Of him, myself, and thee, I am forsaken;
A torment thrice threefold thus to be cross'd.
Prison my heart in thy steel bosom's ward,
But then my friend's heart let my poor heart bail;
Whoe'er keeps me, let my heart be his guard;
Thou canst not then use rigor in my gaol:
    And yet thou wilt; for I, being pent in thee,
    Perforce am thine, and all that is in me.

134

So, now I have confess'd that he is thine,
And I myself am mortgaged to thy will,
Myself I'll forfeit, so that other mine
Thou wilt restore, to be my comfort still:
But thou wilt not, nor he will not be free,
For thou art covetous and he is kind;
He learn'd but surety-like to write for me
Under that bond that him as fast doth bind.
The statute of thy beauty thou wilt take,
Thou usurer, that put'st forth all to use,
And sue a friend came debtor for my sake;
So him I lose through my unkind abuse.
    Him have I lost; thou hast both him and me:
    He pays the whole, and yet am I not free.

135

Whoever hath her wish, thou hast thy 'Will,'
And 'Will' to boot, and 'Will' in overplus;
More than enough am I that vex thee still,
To thy sweet will making addition thus.
Wilt thou, whose will is large and spacious,
Not once vouchsafe to hide my will in thine?
Shall will in others seem right gracious,
And in my will no fair acceptance shine?
The sea, all water, yet receives rain still
And in abundance addeth to his store;
So thou, being rich in 'Will,' add to thy 'Will'
One will of mine, to make thy large 'Will' more.
   Let no unkind, no fair beseechers kill;
    Think all but one, and me in that one 'Will.'

136

If thy soul cheque thee that I come so near,
Swear to thy blind soul that I was thy 'Will,'
And will, thy soul knows, is admitted there;
Thus far for love my love-suit, sweet, fulfil.
'Will' will fulfil the treasure of thy love,
Ay, fill it full with wills, and my will one.
In things of great receipt with ease we prove
Among a number one is reckon'd none:
Then in the number let me pass untold,
Though in thy stores' account I one must be;
For nothing hold me, so it please thee hold
That nothing me, a something sweet to thee:
   Make but my name thy love, and love that still,
    And then thou lovest me, for my name is 'Will.'

137

Thou blind fool, Love, what dost thou to mine eyes,
That they behold, and see not what they see?
They know what beauty is, see where it lies,
Yet what the best is take the worst to be.
If eyes corrupt by over-partial looks
Be anchor'd in the bay where all men ride,
Why of eyes' falsehood hast thou forgèd hooks,
Whereto the judgment of my heart is tied?
Why should my heart think that a several plot
Which my heart knows the wide world's common
    place?
Or mine eyes seeing this, say this is not,
To put fair truth upon so foul a face?
    In things right true my heart and eyes have erred,
    And to this false plague are they now transferr'd.

138

When my love swears that she is made of truth
I do believe her, though I know she lies,
That she might think me some untutor'd youth,
Unlearnèd in the world's false subtleties.
Thus vainly thinking that she thinks me young,
Although she knows my days are past the best,
Simply I credit her false speaking tongue:
On both sides thus is simple truth suppress'd.
But wherefore says she not she is unjust?
And wherefore say not I that I am old?
O, love's best habit is in seeming trust,
And age in love loves not to have years told:
    Therefore I lie with her and she with me,
    And in our faults by lies we flatter'd be.

139

O, call not me to justify the wrong
That thy unkindness lays upon my heart;
Wound me not with thine eye but with thy tongue;
Use power with power and slay me not by art.
Tell me thou lovest elsewhere, but in my sight,
Dear heart, forbear to glance thine eye aside:
What need'st thou wound with cunning when
    thy might
Is more than my o'er-press'd defense can bide?
Let me excuse thee: ah! my love well knows
Her pretty looks have been mine enemies,
And therefore from my face she turns my foes,
That they elsewhere might dart their injuries:
    Yet do not so; but since I am near slain,
    Kill me outright with looks and rid my pain.

140

Be wise as thou art cruel; do not press
My tongue-tied patience with too much disdain;
Lest sorrow lend me words and words express
The manner of my pity-wanting pain.
If I might teach thee wit, better it were,
Though not to love, yet, love, to tell me so;
As testy sick men, when their deaths be near,
No news but health from their physicians know;
For if I should despair, I should grow mad,
And in my madness might speak ill of thee:
Now this ill-wresting world is grown so bad,
Mad slanderers by mad ears believed be,
    That I may not be so, nor thou belied,
    Bear thine eyes straight, though thy proud heart
      go wide.

141

In faith, I do not love thee with mine eyes,
For they in thee a thousand errors note;
But 'tis my heart that loves what they despise,
Who in despite of view is pleased to dote;
Nor are mine ears with thy tongue's tune delighted,
Nor tender feeling, to base touches prone,
Nor taste, nor smell, desire to be invited
To any sensual feast with thee alone:
But my five wits nor my five senses can
Dissuade one foolish heart from serving thee,
Who leaves unsway'd the likeness of a man,
Thy proud hearts slave and vassal wretch to be:
    Only my plague thus far I count my gain,
    That she that makes me sin awards me pain.

142

Love is my sin and thy dear virtue hate,
Hate of my sin, grounded on sinful loving:
O, but with mine compare thou thine own state,
And thou shalt find it merits not reproving;
Or, if it do, not from those lips of thine,
That have profaned their scarlet ornaments
And seal'd false bonds of love as oft as mine,
Robb'd others' beds' revenues of their rents.
Be it lawful I love thee, as thou lovest those
Whom thine eyes woo as mine importune thee:
Root pity in thy heart, that when it grows
Thy pity may deserve to pitied be.
    If thou dost seek to have what thou dost hide,
    By self-example mayst thou be denied!

143

Lo! as a careful housewife runs to catch
One of her feather'd creatures broke away,
Sets down her babe and makes an swift dispatch
In pursuit of the thing she would have stay,
Whilst her neglected child holds her in chase,
Cries to catch her whose busy care is bent
To follow that which flies before her face,
Not prizing her poor infant's discontent;
So runn'st thou after that which flies from thee,
Whilst I thy babe chase thee afar behind;
But if thou catch thy hope, turn back to me,
And play the mother's part, kiss me, be kind:
    So will I pray that thou mayst have thy 'Will,'
    If thou turn back, and my loud crying still.

144

Two loves I have of comfort and despair,
Which like two spirits do suggest me still:
The better angel is a man right fair,
The worser spirit a woman colour'd ill.
To win me soon to hell, my female evil
Tempteth my better angel from my side,
And would corrupt my saint to be a devil,
Wooing his purity with her foul pride.
And whether that my angel be turn'd fiend
Suspect I may, but not directly tell;
But being both from me, both to each friend,
I guess one angel in another's hell:
    Yet this shall I ne'er know, but live in doubt,
    Till my bad angel fire my good one out.

145

Those lips that Love's own hand did make
Breathed forth the sound that said 'I hate'
To me that languish'd for her sake;
But when she saw my woeful state,
Straight in her heart did mercy come,
Chiding that tongue that ever sweet
Was used in giving gentle doom,
And taught it thus anew to greet:
'I hate' she alter'd with an end,
That follow'd it as gentle day
Doth follow night, who like a fiend
From heaven to hell is flown away;
   'I hate' from hate away she threw,
   And saved my life, saying 'not you.'

147

My love is as a fever, longing still
For that which longer nurseth the disease,
Feeding on that which doth preserve the ill,
The uncertain sickly appetite to please.
My reason, the physician to my love,
Angry that his prescriptions are not kept,
Hath left me, and I desperate now approve
Desire is death, which physic did except.
Past cure I am, now reason is past care,
And frantic-mad with evermore unrest;
My thoughts and my discourse as madmen's are,
At random from the truth vainly express'd;
   For I have sworn thee fair and thought thee
      bright,
   Who art as black as hell, as dark as night.

151

Love is too young to know what conscience is;
Yet who knows not conscience is born of love?
Then, gentle cheater, urge not my amiss,
Lest guilty of my faults thy sweet self prove:
For, thou betraying me, I do betray
My nobler part to my gross body's treason;
My soul doth tell my body that he may
Triumph in love; flesh stays no father reason;
But, rising at thy name, doth point out thee
As his triumphant prize. Proud of this pride,
He is contented thy poor drudge to be,
To stand in thy affairs, fall by thy side.
    No want of conscience hold it that I call
    Her 'love' for whose dear love I rise and fall.

The Phoenix and the Turtle

Let the bird of loudest lay,
On the sole Arabian tree,
Herald sad and trumpet be,
To whose sound chaste wings obey.
But thou shrieking harbinger,
Foul precurrer of the fiend,
Augur of the fever's end,
To this troop come thou not near!
From this session interdict
Every fowl of tyrant wing,
Save the eagle, feather'd king:
Keep the obsequy so strict.
Let the priest in surplice white,
That defunctive music can,
Be the death-divining swan,
Lest the requiem lack his right.
And thou treble-dated crow,
That thy sable gender makest
With the breath thou givest and takest,
'Mongst our mourners shalt thou go.
Here the anthem doth commence:
Love and constancy is dead;
Phoenix and the turtle fled
In a mutual flame from hence.
So they loved, as love in twain
Had the essence but in one;
Two distincts, division none:
Number there in love was slain.
Hearts remote, yet not asunder;
Distance, and no space was seen
'Twixt the turtle and his queen:
But in them it were a wonder.
So between them love did shine,
That the turtle saw his right

Flaming in the phoenix' sight;
Either was the other's mine.
Property was thus appalled,
That the self was not the same;
Single nature's double name
Neither two nor one was called.
Reason, in itself confounded,
Saw division grow together,
To themselves yet either neither,
Simple were so well compounded,
That it cried, 'How true a twain
Seemeth this concordant one!
Love hath reason, reason none,
If what parts can so remain.'
Whereupon it made this threne
To the phoenix and the dove,
Co-supremes and stars of love,
As chorus to their tragic scene.

THRENOS

Beauty, truth, and rarity,
Grace in all simplicity,
Here enclosed in cinders lie.
Death is now the phoenix' nest
And the turtle's loyal breast
To eternity doth rest,
Leaving no posterity:
'Twas not their infirmity,
It was married chastity.
Truth may seem, but cannot be:
Beauty brag, but 'tis not she;
Truth and beauty buried be.
To this urn let those repair
That are either true or fair
For these dead birds sigh a prayer.

ISABELLA

  God save your honour!

ANGELO

    [*Aside*]

  From thee, even from thy virtue!
  What's this, what's this? Is this her fault or mine?
  The tempter or the tempted, who sins most? Ha!
  Not she: nor doth she tempt: but it is I
  That, lying by the violet in the sun,
  Do as the carrion does, not as the flower,
  Corrupt with virtuous season. Can it be
  That modesty may more betray our sense
  Than woman's lightness? Having waste ground
      enough,
  Shall we desire to raze the sanctuary
  And pitch our evils there? O, fie, fie, fie!
  What dost thou, or what art thou, Angelo?
  Dost thou desire her foully for those things
  That make her good? O, let her brother live!
  Thieves for their robbery have authority
  When judges steal themselves. What, do I love her,
  That I desire to hear her speak again,
  And feast upon her eyes? What is't I dream on?
  O cunning enemy, that, to catch a saint,
  With saints dost bait thy hook! Most dangerous
  Is that temptation that doth goad us on
  To sin in loving virtue: never could the strumpet,
  With all her double vigour, art and nature,
  Once stir my temper; but this virtuous maid
  Subdues me quite. Even till now,
  When men were fond, I smiled and wonder'd
      how.

                    **From *Measure for Measure*,
                    Act Two, scene 2**

ANGELO

You seem'd of late to make the law a tyrant;
And rather proved the sliding of your brother
A merriment than a vice.

ISABELLA

O, pardon me, my lord; it oft falls out,
To have what we would have, we speak not
what we mean:
I something do excuse the thing I hate,
For his advantage that I dearly love.

ANGELO

We are all frail.

ISABELLA

Else let my brother die,
If not a feodary, but only he
Owe and succeed thy weakness.

ANGELO

Nay, women are frail too.

ISABELLA

Ay, as the glasses where they view themselves;
Which are as easy broke as they make forms.
Women! Help Heaven! men their creation mar
In profiting by them. Nay, call us ten times frail;
For we are soft as our complexions are,
And credulous to false prints.

ANGELO

I think it well:
And from this testimony of your own sex,—
Since I suppose we are made to be no stronger
Than faults may shake our frames—let me be bold;
I do arrest your words. Be that you are,
That is, a woman; if you be more, you're none;
If you be one, as you are well express'd
By all external warrants, show it now,
By putting on the destined livery.

ISABELLA

I have no tongue but one: gentle my lord,
Let me entreat you speak the former language.

ANGELO

Plainly conceive, I love you.

ISABELLA

My brother did love Juliet,
And you tell me that he shall die for it.

ANGELO

He shall not, Isabel, if you give me love.

ISABELLA

I know your virtue hath a licence in't,
Which seems a little fouler than it is,
To pluck on others.

ANGELO

                 Believe me, on mine honour,
My words express my purpose.

ISABELLA

Ha! little honour to be much believed,
And most pernicious purpose! Seeming, seeming!
I will proclaim thee, Angelo; look for't:
Sign me a present pardon for my brother,
Or with an outstretch'd throat I'll tell the world
    aloud
What man thou art.

ANGELO

               Who will believe thee, Isabel?
My unsoil'd name, the austereness of my life,
My vouch against you, and my place i' the state,
Will so your accusation overweigh,
That you shall stifle in your own report
And smell of calumny. I have begun,
And now I give my sensual race the rein:
Fit thy consent to my sharp appetite;
Lay by all nicety and prolixious blushes,
That banish what they sue for; redeem thy
    brother
By yielding up thy body to my will;
Or else he must not only die the death,
But thy unkindness shall his death draw out
To lingering sufferance. Answer me to-morrow,

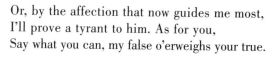

Or, by the affection that now guides me most,
I'll prove a tyrant to him. As for you,
Say what you can, my false o'erweighs your true.

From *Measure for Measure*,
Act Two, scene 4

OTHELLO

Her father loved me; oft invited me;
Still question'd me the story of my life,
From year to year, the battles, sieges, fortunes,
That I have passed.
I ran it through, even from my boyish days,
To the very moment that he bade me tell it;
Wherein I spake of most disastrous chances,
Of moving accidents by flood and field
Of hair-breadth scapes i' the imminent deadly
    breach,
Of being taken by the insolent foe
And sold to slavery, of my redemption thence
And portance in my travels' history:
Wherein of antres vast and deserts idle,
Rough quarries, rocks and hills whose heads
    touch heaven
It was my hint to speak,—such was the
    process;
And of the Cannibals that each other eat,
The Anthropophagi and men whose heads
Do grow beneath their shoulders. This to hear
Would Desdemona seriously incline:
But still the house-affairs would draw her thence:
Which ever as she could with haste dispatch,
She'd come again, and with a greedy ear
Devour up my discourse: which I observing,
Took once a pliant hour, and found good means
To draw from her a prayer of earnest heart
That I would all my pilgrimage dilate,
Whereof by parcels she had something heard,
But not intentively: I did consent,
And often did beguile her of her tears,
When I did speak of some distressful stroke
That my youth suffer'd. My story being done,
She gave me for my pains a world of sighs:
She swore, in faith, 'twas strange, 'twas passing
    strange,

'Twas pitiful, 'twas wondrous pitiful:
She wish'd she had not heard it, yet she wish'd
That heaven had made her such a man: she
     thank'd me,
And bade me, if I had a friend that loved her,
I should but teach him how to tell my story.
And that would woo her. Upon this hint I spake:
She loved me for the dangers I had pass'd,
And I loved her that she did pity them.
This only is the witchcraft I have used:
Here comes the lady; let her witness it.

From *Othello*,
Act One, scene 3

OTHELLO

Excellent wretch! Perdition catch my soul,
But I do love thee! and when I love thee not,
Chaos is come again.

From *Othello*,
Act Three, scene 3

DESDEMONA

My mother had a maid call'd Barbara:
She was in love, and he she loved proved mad
And did forsake her: she had a song of 'willow';
An old thing 'twas, but it express'd her fortune,
And she died singing it: that song to-night
Will not go from my mind; I have much to do,
But to go hang my head all at one side,
And sing it like poor Barbara. Prithee, dispatch.
  . . . .

[*Singing*]

'The poor soul sat sighing by a sycamore tree,
   Sing all a green willow:
Her hand on her bosom, her head on her knee,
   Sing willow, willow, willow:
The fresh streams ran by her, and murmur'd
      her moans;
   Sing willow, willow, willow;
Her salt tears fell from her, and soften'd the
      stones;
   Sing willow'—
Lay by these:—

                        'willow, willow.'

Prithee, hie thee; he'll come anon:—
   [*Singing*]
'Sing all a green willow must be my garland.
Let nobody blame him; his scorn I approve'—
Nay, that's not next.—Hark! who is't that
      knocks?

EMILIA

It's the wind.

DESDEMONA

   [*Singing*]
'I call'd my love false love; but what said he then?
   Sing willow, willow, willow:
If I court more women, you'll couch with more
      men.'
So, get thee gone; good night. Mine eyes do itch;
Doth that bode weeping?

                        From *Othello*,
                        Act Four, scene 2

OTHELLO

It is the cause, it is the cause, my soul,—
Let me not name it to you, you chaste stars!—
It is the cause. Yet I'll not shed her blood;
Nor scar that whiter skin of hers than snow,
And smooth as monumental alabaster.
Yet she must die, else she'll betray more men.
Put out the light, and then put out the light:
If I quench thee, thou flaming minister,
I can again thy former light restore,
Should I repent me: but once put out thy light,
Thou cunning'st pattern of excelling nature,
I know not where is that Promethean heat
That can thy light relume. When I have pluck'd
    the rose,
I cannot give it vital growth again.
It must needs wither: I'll smell it on the tree.
    [*Kissing her*]
Ah balmy breath, that dost almost persuade
Justice to break her sword! One more, one more.
Be thus when thou art dead, and I will kill thee,
And love thee after. One more, and this the last:
So sweet was ne'er so fatal. I must weep,
But they are cruel tears: this sorrow's heavenly;
It strikes where it doth love. She wakes.

    .   .   .   .

OTHELLO

Soft you; a word or two before you go.
I have done the state some service, and they
    know't.
No more of that. I pray you, in your letters,
When you shall these unlucky deeds relate,
Speak of me as I am; nothing extenuate,
Nor set down aught in malice: then must you
    speak
Of one that loved not wisely but too well;
Of one not easily jealous, but being wrought
Perplex'd in the extreme; of one whose hand,

Like the base Indian, threw a pearl away
Richer than all his tribe; of one whose subdued
    eyes,
Albeit unusèd to the melting mood,
Drop tears as fast as the Arabian trees
Their medicinal gum. Set you down this;
And say besides, that in Aleppo once,
Where a malignant and a turban'd Turk
Beat a Venetian and traduced the state,
I took by the throat the circumcisèd dog,
And smote him, thus.
    [*Stabs himself*]

LODOVICO
O bloody period!

GRATIANO
All that's spoke is marr'd.

OTHELLO
I kiss'd thee ere I kill'd thee: no way but this;
Killing myself, to die upon a kiss.
    [*Falls on the bed, and dies*]

**From *Othello*,
Act Five, scene 2**

HELENA
O, were that all! I think not on my father;
And these great tears grace his remembrance
    more
Than those I shed for him. What was he like?
I have forgot him: my imagination
Carries no favour in't but Bertram's.
I am undone: there is no living, none,
If Bertram be away. 'Twere all one
That I should love a bright particular star
And think to wed it, he is so above me:

In his bright radiance and collateral light
Must I be comforted, not in his sphere.
The ambition in my love thus plagues itself:
The hind that would be mated by the lion
Must die for love. 'Twas pretty, though plague,
To see him every hour; to sit and draw
His archèd brows, his hawking eye, his curls,
In our heart's table; heart too capable
Of every line and trick of his sweet favour:
But now he's gone, and my idolatrous fancy
Must sanctify his reliques. Who comes here?
　　[*Enter Parolles*]
One that goes with him: I love him for his sake;
And yet I know him a notorious liar,
Think him a great way fool, solely a coward;
Yet these fixed evils sit so fit in him,
That they take place, when virtue's steely bones
Look bleak i' the cold wind: withal, full oft we see
Cold wisdom waiting on superfluous folly.

PAROLLES

Save you, fair queen!

HELENA

And you, monarch!

PAROLLES

No.

HELENA

And no.

PAROLLES

Are you meditating on virginity?

HELENA

Ay. You have some stain of soldier in you: let
me ask you a question. Man is enemy to vir-
ginity; how may we barricado it against him?

PAROLLES

Keep him out.

HELENA

But he assails; and our virginity, though
valiant, in the defence yet is weak: unfold to
us some warlike resistance.

PAROLLES

There is none: man, sitting down before you, will undermine you and blow you up.

HELENA

Bless our poor virginity from underminers and blowers up! Is there no military policy, how virgins might blow up men?

PAROLLES

Virginity being blown down, man will quicklier be blown up: marry, in blowing him down again, with the breach yourselves made, you lose your city. It is not politic in the commonwealth of nature to preserve virginity. Loss of virginity is rational increase and there was never virgin got till virginity was first lost. That you were made of is metal to make virgins. Virginity by being once lost may be ten times found; by being ever kept, it is ever lost: 'tis too cold a companion; away with 't!

HELENA

I will stand for 't a little, though therefore I die a virgin.

PAROLLES

There's little can be said in 't; 'tis against the rule of nature. To speak on the part of virginity, is to accuse your mothers; which is most infallible disobedience. He that hangs himself is a virgin: virginity murders itself and should be buried in highways out of all sanctified limit, as a desperate offendress against nature. Virginity breeds mites, much like a cheese; consumes itself to the very paring, and so dies with feeding his own stomach. Besides, virginity is peevish, proud, idle, made of self-love, which is the most inhibited sin in the canon. Keep it not; you cannot choose but lose by 't: out with 't! within ten year it will make itself ten, which is a goodly increase; and the prin-

cipal itself not much the worse: away with 't!
HELENA

How might one do, sir, to lose it to her own liking?
PAROLLES

Let me see: marry, ill, to like him that ne'er it
likes. 'Tis a commodity will lose the gloss with
lying; the longer kept, the less worth: off with
't while 'tis vendible; answer the time of
request. Virginity, like an old courtier, wears
her cap out of fashion: richly suited, but
unsuitable: just like the brooch and the tooth-
pick, which wear not now. Your date is better
in your pie and your porridge than in your
cheek; and your virginity, your old virginity, is
like one of our French withered pears, it looks
ill, it eats drily; marry, 'tis a withered pear; it
was formerly better; marry, yet 'tis a withered
pear: will you anything with it?
HELENA

Not my virginity yet . . .
There shall your master have a thousand loves,
A mother and a mistress and a friend,
A phoenix, captain and an enemy,
A guide, a goddess, and a sovereign,
A counsellor, a traitress, and a dear;
His humble ambition, proud humility,
His jarring concord, and his discord dulcet,
His faith, his sweet disaster; with a world
Of pretty, fond, adoptious christendoms,
That blinking Cupid gossips. Now shall he—
I know not what he shall. God send him well!
The court's a learning place, and he is one—
PAROLLES

What one, i' faith?
HELENA

That I wish well. 'Tis pity—
PAROLLES

What's pity?

HELENA

That wishing well had not a body in't,
Which might be felt; that we, the poorer born,
Whose baser stars do shut us up in wishes,
Might with effects of them follow our friends,
And show what we alone must think, which never
Return us thanks.

From *All's Well That Ends Well*,
Act One, scene 1

PHILO

    Nay, but this dotage of our general's
    O'erflows the measure: those his goodly eyes,
    That o'er the files and musters of the war
    Have glow'd like plated Mars, now bend, now turn,
    The office and devotion of their view
    Upon a tawny front: his captain's heart,
    Which in the scuffles of great fights hath burst
    The buckles on his breast, reneges all temper,
    And is become the bellows and the fan
    To cool a gipsy's lust.

    *[Flourish. Enter Antony, Cleopatra, her
    Ladies, the Train, with Eunuchs fanning her]*
                   Look, where they come:
    Take but good note, and you shall see in him.
    The triple pillar of the world transform'd
    Into a strumpet's fool: behold and see.

CLEOPATRA

    If it be love indeed, tell me how much.

ANTONY

    There's beggary in the love that can be reckon'd.

CLEOPATRA

    I'll set a bourn how far to be beloved.

ANTONY

    Then must thou needs find out new heaven, new earth.

    [Enter an Attendant]

ATTENDANT

    News, my good lord, from Rome.

ANTONY

    Grates me: the sum.

CLEOPATRA

                   Nay, hear them, Antony:
    Fulvia perchance is angry; or, who knows
    If the scarce-bearded Caesar have not sent
    His powerful mandate to you, 'Do this, or this;
    Take in that kingdom, and enfranchise that;
    Perform 't, or else we damn thee.'

ANTONY

How, my love!

CLEOPATRA

Perchance! nay, and most like:
You must not stay here longer, your dismission
Is come from Caesar; therefore hear it, Antony.
Where's Fulvia's process? Caesar's I would
  say? both?
Call in the messengers. As I am Egypt's queen,
Thou blushest, Antony; and that blood of thine
Is Caesar's homager: else so thy cheek pays
  shame
When shrill-tongued Fulvia scolds. The
  messengers!

ANTONY

Let Rome in Tiber melt, and the wide arch
Of the ranged empire fall! Here is my space.
Kingdoms are clay: our dungy earth alike
Feeds beast as man: the nobleness of life
Is to do thus; when such a mutual pair
  [*Embracing*]
And such a twain can do't, in which I bind,
On pain of punishment, the world to weet
We stand up peerless.

CLEOPATRA

Excellent falsehood!
Why did he marry Fulvia, and not love her?
I'll seem the fool I am not; Antony
Will be himself.

ANTONY

But stirr'd by Cleopatra.
Now, for the love of Love and her soft hours,
Let's not confound the time with conference
  harsh:
There's not a minute of our lives should stretch
Without some pleasure now. What sport tonight?

CLEOPATRA

Hear the ambassadors.

ANTONY

Fie, wrangling queen!
Whom every thing becomes, to chide, to laugh,
To weep; whose every passion fully strives
To make itself, in thee, fair and admired!
No messenger, but thine; and all alone
To-night we'll wander through the streets and
note
The qualities of people. Come, my queen;
Last night you did desire it: speak not to us.

From *Antony and Cleopatra*,
Act One, scene 1

ANTONY

I must with haste from hence.

ENOBARBUS

Why, then, we kill all our women: we see how
mortal an unkindness is to them; if they suffer
our departure, death's the word.

ANTONY

I must be gone.

ENOBARBUS

Under a compelling occasion, let women die; it
were pity to cast them away for nothing;
though, between them and a great cause, they
should be esteemed nothing. Cleopatra, catch-
ing but the least noise of this, dies instantly; I
have seen her die twenty times upon far poor-
er moment: I do think there is mettle in death,
which commits some loving act upon her, she
hath such a celerity in dying.

ANTONY

She is cunning past man's thought.

ENOBARBUS

Alack, sir, no; her passions are made of nothing but the finest part of pure love: we cannot call her winds and waters sighs and tears; they are greater storms and tempests than almanacs can report: this cannot be cunning in her; if it be, she makes a shower of rain as well as Jove.

ANTONY

Would I had never seen her.

ENOBARBUS

O, sir, you had then left unseen a wonderful piece of work; which not to have been blest withal would have discredited your travel.

**From *Antony and Cleopatra*,
Act One, scene 2**

CLEOPATRA

Charmian!

CHARMIAN

Madam?

CLEOPATRA

Ha, ha! Give me to drink mandragora.

CHARMIAN

Why, madam?

CLEOPATRA

That I might sleep out this great gap of time
My Antony is away.

CHARMIAN

               You think of him too much.

CLEOPATRA

O, 'tis treason!

CHARMIAN

           Madam, I trust, not so.

CLEOPATRA
Thou, eunuch Mardian!
MARDIAN
What's your highness' pleasure?
CLEOPATRA
Not now to hear thee sing; I take no pleasure
In aught an eunuch has: 'tis well for thee,
That, being unseminar'd, thy freer thoughts
May not fly forth of Egypt. Hast thou affections?
MARDIAN
Yes, gracious madam.
CLEOPATRA
Indeed!
MARDIAN
Not in deed, madam; for I can do nothing
But what indeed is honest to be done:
Yet have I fierce affections, and think
What Venus did with Mars.
CLEOPATRA
O Charmian,
Where think'st thou he is now? Stands he, or
sits he?
Or does he walk? or is he on his horse?
O happy horse, to bear the weight of Antony!
Do bravely, horse! for wot'st thou whom thou
movest?
The demi-Atlas of this earth, the arm
And burgonet of men. He's speaking now,
Or murmuring 'Where's my serpent of old Nile?'
For so he calls me: now I feed myself
With most delicious poison. Think on me,
That am with Phoebus' amorous pinches black,
And wrinkled deep in time? Broad-fronted
Caesar,
When thou wast here above the ground, I was
A morsel for a monarch: and great Pompey
Would stand and make his eyes grow in my brow;
There would he anchor his aspect and die

With looking on his life.

[*Enter Alexas, from Octavius Caesar*]

ALEXAS

Sovereign of Egypt, hail!

CLEOPATRA

How much unlike art thou Mark Antony!
Yet, coming from him, that great medicine hath
With his tinct gilded thee.
How goes it with my brave Mark Antony?

ALEXAS

Last thing he did, dear queen,
He kiss'd,—the last of many doubled kisses,—
This orient pearl. His speech sticks in my heart.

CLEOPATRA

Mine ear must pluck it thence.

ALEXAS

'Good friend,' quoth he,
'Say, the firm Roman to great Egypt sends
This treasure of an oyster; at whose foot,
To mend the petty present, I will piece
Her opulent throne with kingdoms; all the east,
Say thou, shall call her mistress.' So he nodded,
And soberly did mount an arm-gaunt steed,
Who neigh'd so high, that what I would have
        spoke
Was beastly dumb'd by him.

CLEOPATRA

What, was he sad or merry?

ALEXAS

Like to the time o' the year between the
        extremes
Of hot and cold, he was nor sad nor merry.

CLEOPATRA

O well-divided disposition! Note him,
Note him good Charmian, 'tis the man; but
        note him:
He was not sad, for he would shine on those
That make their looks by his; he was not merry,

Which seem'd to tell them his remembrance lay
In Egypt with his joy; but between both:
O heavenly mingle! Be'st thou sad or merry,
The violence of either thee becomes,
So does it no man else. Met'st thou my posts?

ALEXAS

Ay, madam, twenty several messengers:
Why do you send so thick?

CLEOPATRA

Who's born that day
When I forget to send to Antony,
Shall die a beggar. Ink and paper, Charmian.
Welcome, my good Alexas. Did I, Charmian,
Ever love Caesar so?

CHARMIAN

O that brave Caesar!

CLEOPATRA

Be choked with such another emphasis!
Say, the brave Antony.

CHARMIAN

The valiant Caesar!

CLEOPATRA

By Isis, I will give thee bloody teeth,
If thou with Caesar paragon again
My man of men.

CHARMIAN

By your most gracious pardon,
I sing but after you.

CLEOPATRA

My salad days,
When I was green in judgment: cold in blood,
To say as I said then! But, come, away;
Get me ink and paper:
He shall have every day a several greeting,
Or I'll unpeople Egypt.

**From _Antony and Cleopatra_,
Act One, scene 5**

MECAENAS

    She's a most triumphant lady, if report be square
to her.

ENOBARBUS

    When she first met Mark Antony, she pursed
up his heart, upon the river of Cydnus.

AGRIPPA

    There she appeared indeed; or my reporter
devised well for her.

ENOBARBUS

    I will tell you.
    The barge she sat in, like a burnish'd throne,
    Burn'd on the water: the poop was beaten gold;
    Purple the sails, and so perfumèd that
    The winds were love-sick with them; the oars
         were silver,
    Which to the tune of flutes kept stroke, and made
    The water which they beat to follow faster,
    As amorous of their strokes. For her own person,
    It beggar'd all description: she did lie
    In her pavilion—cloth-of-gold of tissue—
    O'er-picturing that Venus where we see
    The fancy outwork nature: on each side her
    Stood pretty dimpled boys, like smiling Cupids,
    With divers-colour'd fans, whose wind did seem
    To glow the delicate cheeks which they did cool,
    And what they undid did.

AGRIPPA

                    O, rare for Antony!

ENOBARBUS

    Her gentlewomen, like the Nereides,
    So many mermaids, tended her i' the eyes,
    And made their bends adornings: at the helm
    A seeming mermaid steers: the silken tackle
    Swell with the touches of those flower-soft hands,
    That yarely frame the office. From the barge
    A strange invisible perfume hits the sense
    Of the adjacent wharfs. The city cast

Her people out upon her; and Antony,
Enthroned i' the market-place, did sit alone,
Whistling to the air; which, but for vacancy,
Had gone to gaze on Cleopatra too,
And made a gap in nature.

AGRIPPA

                    Rare Egyptian!

ENOBARBUS
Upon her landing, Antony sent to her,
Invited her to supper: she replied,
It should be better he became her guest;
Which she entreated: our courteous Antony,
Whom ne'er the word of 'No' woman heard speak,
Being barber'd ten times o'er, goes to the feast,
And for his ordinary pays his heart
For what his eyes eat only.

AGRIPPA

                    Royal wench!
She made great Caesar lay his sword to bed:
He plough'd her, and she cropp'd.

ENOBARBUS

                         I saw her once
Hop forty paces through the public street;
And having lost her breath, she spoke, and panted,
That she did make defect perfection,
And, breathless, power breathe forth.

MECAENAS

                    Now Antony
Must leave her utterly.

ENOBARBUS

              Never; he will not:
Age cannot wither her, nor custom stale
Her infinite variety: other women cloy
The appetites they feed: but she makes hungry
Where most she satisfies; for vilest things
Become themselves in her: that the holy priests
Bless her when she is riggish.

From *Antony and Cleopatra*,
Act Two, scene 2

ANTONY

O, whither hast thou led me, Egypt? See,
How I convey my shame out of thine eyes
By looking back what I have left behind
'Stroy'd in dishonour.

CLEOPATRA

         O my lord, my lord,
Forgive my fearful sails! I little thought
You would have follow'd.

ANTONY

         Egypt, thou knew'st too well
My heart was to thy rudder tied by the strings,
And thou shouldst tow me after: o'er my spirit
Thy full supremacy thou knew'st, and that
Thy beck might from the bidding of the gods
Command me.

CLEOPATRA

      O, my pardon!

ANTONY

        Now I must
To the young man send humble treaties, dodge
And palter in the shifts of lowness; who
With half the bulk o' the world play'd as I pleased,
Making and marring fortunes. You did know
How much you were my conqueror; and that
My sword, made weak by my affection, would
Obey it on all cause.

CLEOPATRA

       Pardon, pardon!

ANTONY

Fall not a tear, I say; one of them rates
All that is won and lost: give me a kiss;
Even this repays me. We sent our schoolmaster;
Is he come back? Love, I am full of lead.
Some wine, within there, and our viands!
     Fortune knows
We scorn her most when most she offers blows.

            From *Antony and Cleopatra*,
                Act Three, scene 11

[Enter, below, Mark Antony, borne by the Guard]

CLEOPATRA

                                  O sun,

Burn the great sphere thou movest in! darkling stand

The varying shore o' the world. O Antony,

Antony, Antony! Help, Charmian,

Help, Iras, help; help, friends below;

Let's draw him hither.

ANTONY

                          Peace! Not Caesar's valour

Hath o'erthrown Antony, but Antony's

Hath triumph'd on itself.

CLEOPATRA

                      So it should be,

That none but Antonys should conquer Antony.

But woe 'tis so!

ANTONY

I am dying, Egypt, dying; only

I here importune death awhile, until

Of many thousand kisses the poor last

I lay up thy lips.

CLEOPATRA

                I dare not, dear,—

Dear my lord, pardon,—I dare not,

Lest I be taken: not the imperious show

Of the full-fortuned Caesar ever shall

Be brooch'd with me; if knife, drugs, serpents, have

Edge, sting, or operation, I am safe:

Your wife Octavia, with her modest eyes

And still conclusion, shall acquire no honour

Demuring upon me. But come, come, Antony,—

Help me, my women,—we must draw thee up:

Assist, good friends.

ANTONY

                O, quick, or I am gone.

CLEOPATRA

Here's sport indeed! How heavy weighs my lord!

Our strength is all gone into heaviness,
That makes the weight: had I great Juno's power,
The strong-wing'd Mercury should fetch thee up,
And set thee by Jove's side. Yet come a little,—
Wishes were ever fools,—O, come, come, come;

[*They heave Mark Antony aloft to Cleopatra*]

And welcome, welcome! die where thou hast
    lived:
Quicken with kissing: had my lips that power,
Thus would I wear them out.

ALL   A heavy sight!

ANTONY

I am dying, Egypt, dying:
Give me some wine, and let me speak a little.

CLEOPATRA

No, let me speak; and let me rail so high,
That the false housewife Fortune break her
    wheel,
Provoked by my offence.

ANTONY

                     One word, sweet queen:
Of Caesar seek your honour, with your safety. O!

CLEOPATRA

They do not go together.

ANTONY:

                     Gentle, hear me:
None about Caesar trust but Proculeius.

CLEOPATRA

My resolution and my hands I'll trust;
None about Caesar.

ANTONY

The miserable change now at my end
Lament nor sorrow at; but please your thoughts
In feeding them with those my former fortunes
Wherein I lived, the greatest prince o' the world,
The noblest; and do now not basely die,
Not cowardly put off my helmet to
My countryman,—a Roman by a Roman

Valiantly vanquish'd. Now my spirit is going;
I can no more.

CLEOPATRA

　　　　　　Noblest of men, woo't die?
Hast thou no care of me? shall I abide
In this dull world, which in thy absence is
No better than a sty? O, see, my women,
　　[*Mark Antony dies*]
The crown o' the earth doth melt. My lord!
O, wither'd is the garland of the war,
The soldier's pole is fall'n: young boys and girls
Are level now with men; the odds is gone,
And there is nothing left remarkable
Beneath the visiting moon.
　　[*Faints*]

CHARMIAN

O, quietness, lady!

IRAS

She is dead too, our sovereign.

CHARMIAN

Lady!

IRAS

Madam!

CHARMIAN

O madam, madam, madam!

IRAS

Royal Egypt, Empress!

CHARMIAN

　　　　　　　　Peace, peace, Iras!

CLEOPATRA

No more, but e'en a woman, and commanded
By such poor passion as the maid that milks
And does the meanest chares. It were for me
To throw my sceptre at the injurious gods;
To tell them that this world did equal theirs
Till they had stol'n our jewel. All's but naught;
Patience is scottish, and impatience does
Become a dog that's mad: then is it sin

To rush into the secret house of death,
Ere death dare come to us? How do you, women?
What, what! good cheer! Why, how now,
        Charmian!
My noble girls! Ah, women, women, look,
Our lamp is spent, it's out! Good sirs, take heart:
We'll bury him; and then, what's brave, what's
        noble,
Let's do it after the high Roman fashion,
And make death proud to take us. Come, away:
This case of that huge spirit now is cold:
Ah, women, women! come; we have no friend
But resolution, and the briefest end.

From *Antony and Cleopatra*,
Act Four, scene 16

CLEOPATRA

    Give me my robe, put on my crown; I have
    Immortal longings in me: now no more
    The juice of Egypt's grape shall moist this lip:
    Yare, yare, good Iras; quick. Methinks I hear
    Antony call; I see him rouse himself
    To praise my noble act; I hear him mock
    The luck of Caesar, which the gods give men
    To excuse their after wrath: husband, I come:
    Now to that name my courage prove my title!
    I am fire and air; my other elements
    I give to baser life. So; have you done?
    Come then, and take the last warmth of my lips.
    Farewell, kind Charmian; Iras, long farewell.
      [*Kisses them. Iras falls and dies*]
    Have I the aspic in my lips? Dost fall?
    If thou and nature can so gently part,
    The stroke of death is as a lover's pinch,
    Which hurts, and is desired. Dost thou lie still?
    If thus thou vanishest, thou tell'st the world
    It is not worth leave-taking.

CHARMIAN

    Dissolve, thick cloud, and rain; that I may say,
    The gods themselves do weep!

CLEOPATRA

                 This proves me base:
    If she first meet the curlèd Antony,
    He'll make demand of her, and spend that kiss
    Which is my heaven to have. Come, thou mortal
        wretch,
      [*To an asp, which she applies to her breast*]
    With thy sharp teeth this knot intrinsicate
    Of life at once untie: poor venomous fool
    Be angry, and dispatch. O, couldst thou speak,
    That I might hear thee call great Caesar ass
    Unpolicied!

CHARMIAN

        O eastern star!

CLEOPATRA

Peace, peace!
Dost thou not see my baby at my breast,
That sucks the nurse asleep?

CHARMIAN

O, break! O, break!

CLEOPATRA

As sweet as balm, as soft as air, as gentle,—
O Antony!—Nay, I will take thee too.
  [*Applying another asp to her arm*]
What should I stay—
  [*Dies*]

**From *Antony and Cleopatra*,
Act Five, scene 2**

Index of Excerpts from the Plays

Index of Miscellaneous Poems

Index of First Lines of Sonnets